WITHDRAWN

For Reference

Not to be taken from this room

AMERICAN CITIES CHRONOLOGY SERIES

NEW ORLEANS
A CHRONOLOGICAL & DOCUMENTARY HISTORY

1539 - 1970

Compiled and Edited by
MARTIN SIEGEL

Series Editor
HOWARD B. FURER

1975
OCEANA PUBLICATIONS, INC.
Dobbs Ferry, New York

Ref
F
379
,N557
S53

Library of Congress Cataloging in Publication Data

Siegel, Martin, 1928-   comp.
  New Orleans : a chronological and documentary history, 1539-1970.

  (American cities chronology series)
  Bibliography: p.
  1. New Orleans--History--Chronology. 2. New Orleans --History--Sources. I. Title.
F379.N557S53   976.3'35   75-4578
ISBN 0-379-00601-4

© Copyright 1975 by Oceana Publications, Inc.

All rights reserved. No part of this publication may be reproduced or transmitted in any form or by any means, electronic or mechanical, including photocopy, recording, xerography, or any information storage and retrieval system, without permission in writing from the publisher.

Manufactured in the United States of America

TABLE OF CONTENTS

EDITOR'S FOREWORD. v

CHRONOLOGY
    Colonial New Orleans under France and Spain, 1539-1803 . . .   1
    The Americanization of New Orleans: Louisiana Purchase
      to the Civil War, 1804-1861   9
    New Orleans from the Civil War to World War I: Growth
      of a Southern Commercial Metropolis, 1862-1914   23
    New Orleans Between Two Wars: Development of a Southern
      Regional Center, 1915-1945   37
    New Orleans Since World War II: A Historical City in
      Contemporary America, 1945-1970   44

DOCUMENTS 59
    New Orleans: From Empire to Municipality: 1539-1718 60
    The "Black Code" of Louisiana, 1724 63
    The Treaty of Paris, 1803: Louisiana Purchase. 66
    The Americanization of New Orleans, 1803-1804 69
    Benjamin Henry Latrobe's Impressions of New Orleans, 1818 . 73
    A View of New Orleans, 1835 76
    Two Seasons at the St. Charles Theatre, 1841 and 1845 . . . 78
    A Dinner at the St. Charles Hotel, 1846 81
    A New Yorker Visits New Orleans, 1850 83
    The City Charter of 1852: Provisions for Funding the Debt. . 85
    The Great Yellow Fever Epidemic of 1853 87
    The Will of Judah Touro, New Orleans Philanthropist, 1854 . 90
    The New Orleans Mardi Gras Begins, 1857 95
    General Butler Takes Command of New Orleans, 1862 97
    Federal Responses to the Mechanics Institute Race Riots,
      1866. 99
    Sanitary Ordinances of New Orleans, June 25, 1879 103
    Report on the Sanitary Conditions of the City, 1882 105
    Mark Twain Arrives in New Orleans, 1883 109
    Business "Boosters," 1894 111
    The Second District Invites Tourists to its French Market,
      1912. 115
    The Birth of the Blues in New Orleans before 1917 117
    The Old Houses of the Vieux Carré, 1937 119
    Reforming the Police Department, 1946 122
    City Planning for Metropolitan New Orleans, 1948 125
    The "Home Rule" Charter of New Orleans, 1954 127
    The New Orleans School Crisis of 1960 130
    Plan to Preserve the Vieux Carré, 1968 135

BIBLIOGRAPHY 139

NAME INDEX 151

EDITOR'S FOREWORD

In compiling this book I have kept in mind that its primary purpose is to introduce the student to the history of the city of New Orleans and then to aid him in undertaking further research on his own.

The chronology, in the first section of the book, provides the basic configurations of the history of the city. Although every care was taken to record the most accurate dates, in cases of conflict I have used the most probable dates. But the student concerned with some question of accuracy is urged to consult the original sources.

The annotated documents included in the second section of the book were selected in the hope that they would increase the student's interest in scholarly research. If what I have chosen stimulates the reader to utilize the bibliography in the third section, then I would consider my labors adequately rewarded.

                                          Martin Siegel
                                          Kean College of New Jersey
                                          Union, New Jersey

CHRONOLOGY

COLONIAL NEW ORLEANS UNDER FRANCE AND SPAIN
1539-1803

1539-1541   Hernando de Soto, heading an expedition from Spain, discovered the Mississippi River. While moving down this river de Soto died on May 21, 1542 and was buried near the mouth of the Red River.

1543   July. Luis Moscoso and the survivors of de Soto's expedition, descending the river on their way to Mexico, were the first Europeans to view the site of the future city.

1682   March 31. Robert Cavelier, Sieur de La Salle, and Henri de Tonti, on their trip from the Great Lakes to the Gulf, stopped at an Indian village at or near present-day New Orleans.

April 9. La Salle erected a cross and a column a short distance from the mouth of the Mississippi and named the territory "Louisiana" in honor of his sovereign and patron Louis XIV of France.

1699   March 6. Pierre Lemoyne, Sieur d'Iberville, and his scouting expedition stopped at the present site of New Orleans where a buffalo was killed, a cross erected, and some trees marked.

1718   Spring. Jean Baptiste Lemoyne, Sieur de Bienville, with the assistance of Adrien de Pauger and Pièrre Blond de la Tour, laid out the streets and founded La Nouvelle Orleans, named in honor of the Regent of France, Philippe, Duc d'Orleans.

1718-1720   Wild speculation in the shares of the Mississippi Company, under the presidency of the financial wizard John Law, advisor to Louis XV, took place.

1719   The French ships <u>Duc du Maine</u> and <u>Aurore</u> brought 500 slaves from Africa to the colony through New Orleans.

1720   The Jesuit historian and missionary Father Charlevoix, wrote a letter to Duchesse de Lesdiguieres, describing the great advantages of the geographical location of New Orleans with reference to the sea routes to Mexico, Havana, and the English colonies.

John Law's "Mississippi Bubble" collapsed, bringing widespread financial disaster. But Law's boom left behind it a significant increase in shipping and speculative finance, greatly affecting the growth of New Orleans.

1721　March. Adrien de Pauger and Pierre le Blond de la Tour completed the layout of New Orleans on the basis of sixty-four squares with the Place d'Armes at the center. Each settler was given a lot 260 feet deep, measured from the river, with frontage of 130 feet. Each square was surrounded by drainage ditches to deal with the fact that the city was below water level, and subject to an overflow of the Mississippi every spring.

The population of the city was 1,256, of which one-half were slaves and fifty Indians.

1722　July 2. The French engineers Pierre Blond de la Tour and Adrien de Pauger, in their ship <u>Adventurier</u>, proved decisively that the port of New Orleans was ideally suited for the docking of large ships and open to inland water transportation to New Biloxi, Mobile, and other colonial settlements to the north.

August. Under Governor Bienville, New Orleans became the capital of Louisiana.

1723　December. Father Charlevoix visited New Orleans and reported that it contained 100 houses, mostly cabins.

1724　March. Governor Bienville promulgated the <u>Code Noir</u> (Black Code) regulating slavery and religious worship in the colony; intermarriage of white settlers with blacks was forbidden, including the right to hold blacks as concubines; Catholicism was the only legal religion and Jews were ordered out of the colony.

1726　Etienne de Perier became governor of the colony.

1727　August 6-7. The Ursulines arrived from France and set up a convent school for girls and facilities for a hospital.

1728　A well-known map shows New Orleans was protected by a levee, and laid out in rectangular lines with eleven squares on the waterfront, and a depth of six squares.

December. The first company of <u>filles à la cassette</u> (girls

	with their trousseaux) arrived and were placed in the care of the Ursuline nuns, while being courted by colonists in need of wives.
1729	December. New Orleans was hastily fortified with ditches and a stockade following receipt of news that the French at Fort Rosalie (Natchez) had been massacred by the Natchez Indians.
1730	French soldiers under Governor Perier, with the assistance of the Choctaw Indians, severely defeated the Natchez near Sicily Island.
1731	The Mississippi Company gave up its charter, and Louisiana became a crown colony under Louis XV.
1731-1742	Bienville was appointed governor of Louisiana for a second term.
1732	May 7. A new superior council was formed under Bienville, made up of the governor general of New France, the town mayor of New Orleans, six councillors, one attorney general, and a clerk.
1735	November 16. A sailor by the name of Jean Louis died and left his savings for the establishment of the first charity hospital in New Orleans.
1741	Cotton was introduced as a crop on Louisiana plantations.
1742	August. Growth of trade prompted the issue of royal letters to the effect that the governor appoint four new assessors for four-year terms.
1743-1753	A Canadian nobleman, Pierre Cavagnal, Marquis de Vaudreuil, was appointed governor; his residence was transformed into a gay and lavish center of social life for the city. Governor Vaudreuil drew up a set of regulations aimed at controlling vice on the New Orleans waterfront.
1751	Jesuits brought sugar cane to the colony and were granted a plantation that became the First District of New Orleans.
1753	A theatrical production, _Le Père Indian_ by Le Blanc Villeneuve, was presented by amateurs at the governor's mansion in New Orleans.

1753-1762	The French naval captain, Louis Billouard de Kerlerec, was made governor. His decade in office was filled with the strains of the French and Indian Wars and increasing rivalries between Capuchin and Jesuit priests.
1763	February 6. Louisiana was ceded to Spain by the Treaty of Paris, together with the city of New Orleans and "the island on which it stands." The Florida parishes and the port of Mobile were ceded to England, thus terminating the Seven Years' War. July 9. The Jesuits were expelled from Louisiana by the French authorities, and their property was confiscated.
1764	A.M. Braud received an exclusive privilege from the French crown to establish a printing press and sell books in New Orleans.
1764	October. The New Orleans inhabitants, shaken by news of the secret transfer of their colony to Spain, sent their wealthiest merchant, Jean Milhet, to France in order to petition the crown to disavow Spanish control of their city.
1765	January. About 650 Acadian refugees from Nova Scotia arrived at New Orleans. They established properous agricultural communities on lands west of the city.
1768	Don Antonio de Ulloa, distinguished scientist and friend of Newton and Voltaire, arrived to take control of Louisiana in the name of Spain. Opposition to Spanish rule in New Orleans broke into open rebellion when a group of insurgents took over the city, and Governor Ulloa sailed for Cuba, leaving the colony for ten months without a European government. October. Braud, crown printer, printed a long memoir summarizing the grievances of the planters and merchants of the colony. It was widely read in Europe.
1769	August 18. The Spanish General Alexander O'Reilly arrived with a flotilla and 4,500 soldiers and took control of the city. Fall. Six leaders of the rebellion were executed and seven were imprisoned. The Superior Council was abolished and a new council, the cabildo, was formed. December 1. The first meeting of the cabildo was held at

New Orleans, composed of the governor, six perpetual regidors, two judges, an attorney general, and a clerk.

1770   February 22. A proclamation of the cabildo assigned a comprehensive schedule of annual taxes upon the city. Anchorage duties were established on every vessel to pay for levee repairs, and special taxes were placed on taverns, billiard tables, coffee houses, butchers, and brandy.

October. Don Luis de Unzaga succeeded Alexander O'Reilly as governor and head of the cabildo.

1776   Oliver Pollack, an agent of the Continental Congress at New Orleans, was permitted by the cabildo to send supplies to George Rogers Clark and other American patriots fighting against the British.

1777   February 1. Don Bernardo de Galvez, twenty-one year old son of the Viceroy of Mexico and nephew of the president of the Council of the Indies, became governor of New Orleans.

1778   Merchants of Boston and other colonial cities were permitted to trade freely at New Orleans under de Galvez.

1779   September 22. Spain declared war against Great Britain, and New Orleans was mobilized to assist the American colonies in their struggle for independence. A Spanish force under Galvez wrested Baton Rouge from the British, and by 1781, all of the Gulf coast country was in Spanish hands.

1785   Don Estevan Miro succeeded Galvez as governor at New Orleans.

1788   March 21. The first great fire destroyed 856 houses, including the cathedral, the convent of the Capuchins, the arsenal, and the prison.

December 5. Padre Antonio de Sedella, later known as "Père Antoine," was appointed commissary of the Inquisition, and upon attempting to establish the tribunal (which had remained dormant since O'Reilly authorized it in 1770), was sent back to Spain by Governor Miro.

December 14. Charles III of Spain died and was succeeded by the weak and incompetent Charles IV.

1791	Refugees from an insurrection in San Domingo arrived in New Orleans. Among them was Louis Tabary and his company of actors who presented the first professional theatrical productions in New Orleans reenforcing French cultural traditions in the nominally Spanish colony.

December 30. Baron de Carondelet succeeded Miro and introduced many reforms in New Orleans, including public lighting and the use of watchmen. A tax of one dollar and twelve and a half cents was placed on every chimney in the city to pay for these improvements. |
| 1792 | October 4. A theater on St. Peter Street opened. |
| 1793 | January 2. News of the execution of Louis XVI led to a declaration of war by the Spanish on the French revolutionaries. Loyalties in New Orleans were split three ways: towards Spain, towards the ancien régime of the Bourbons, and towards the Republicans. Revolutionary songs were sung in New Orleans' theaters, taverns, and streets, while Governor de Carondelet prohibited all gatherings and arrested six "Jacobins" whom he sent to Havana, where they were imprisoned for twelve months.

February 10. The Treaty of Paris broke French power in North America. France was forced to cede to the British all possessions in Canada and the eastern half of Louisiana, with the exception of New Orleans, which was turned over to Spain, along with the western half of Louisiana. This territory remained under Spanish control until 1800, when it was returned to France by the secret Treaty of Ildefonso.

April 25. Pope Pius VI formed the Diocese of Louisiana of which New Orleans became the center, thus reducing the significance and size of the Diocese of Havana. |
| 1794 | St. Louis Cathedral was completed after two churches on the same site had been destroyed by fire.

Le Moniteur de la Louisiane, the first regular newspaper in the colony, a weekly, was founded at New Orleans by a refugee printer from Santo Domingo, Louis Duclot.

March 30. The First Freemason lodge called Loge Parfaite Union No. 29 was installed at New Orleans by several French residents. |

	December 8. A second great fire, almost as destructive as that of 1788, consumed 212 of the newest and best buildings, but not the newly constructed cathedral. Henceforth, premiums were offered to all citizens who would rebuild their roofs with tiles rather than wood shingles. Rebuilding began immediately under such Spanish architects as Don Andres Almonester.
1794-1795	Etienne de Boré perfected a granulation process for manufacturing sugar creating an important staple of New Orleans trade replacing indigo which had declined in importance due to an insect that attacked its plant and could not be controlled.
1795	The Cabildo Palace was erected in New Orleans to house the Spanish colonial administration.
	The Carondelet Canal, connecting the city with the Bayou St. John, was completed by slave laborers contributed by planters.
	October 27. The Pinckney Treaty between the United States and Spain established commercial relations and set the northern boundary of West Florida, ultimately the state line east of the Mississippi, at 31°. Americans were granted free navigation of the Mississippi and Western farmers the "right of deposit" at New Orleans, which Spain withdrew in 1802, precipitating the atmosphere which led to the Louisiana Purchase.
1796	There were eighty lamps to light the streets of New Orleans, and thirteen serenos (watchmen) who formed the police force.
	The first yellow fever epidemic broke out in New Orleans.
	May 22. The opera <u>Sylvain</u> by André Grétry was the first opera performed by professionals in New Orleans.
1797	The Pope put East and West Florida under the authority of Don Louis de Penalvert at the new See of St. Louis Cathedral in New Orleans.
	August 1. Don Manuel Gayoso de Lemos succeeded Baron de Carondelet at the Cabildo.
1798	The Duc d'Orléans visited New Orleans with his brothers, the Duc Montpensier and the Comte Beaujolais. One of their

hosts at New Orleans, Pierre de Marigny, lent the future Louis Philippe of France a large sum of money that was later repaid in the form of educating Marigny's son in France.

The Spanish intendant, Morales, closed the port of New Orleans, but strong protests resulted in the reopening of the port, bringing various projects to capture New Orleans by Americans to a halt.

1799 The Hôtel d'Orléans, the first elaborate New Orleans hotel, was opened to the public.

July 25. Governor Gayso de Lemos died; he was succeeded by the two last Spanish governors Casa Calvo (1799-1801) and Don Juan Manuel de Sacedo.

1801 Judah Touro, the son of a rabbi, arrived at New Orleans penniless at the age of twenty-one. He was destined to become one of the richest merchants and benefactors of New Orleans by the time of his death in 1854.

October 1. The secret Treaty of St. Ildefonso ceded Louisiana back to France.

1803 March. The French colonial prefect, Pierre Laussat, established a new municipal government for New Orleans in place of the cabildo. It was composed of a mayor, two adjuncts, and ten members of the council.

April 30. Napoleon I ceded Louisiana to the United States for eighty million francs, of which twenty million were set aside to pay claims by American citizens against France pending since 1800.

November 30. France took formal possession of the colony from Spain in the Place d'Armes, although Napoleon had already ceded it to the United States. Etienne De Boré became mayor.

December 20. William C.C. Claiborne and General James Wilkinson took possession of Louisiana at New Orleans in the name of the United States.

THE AMERICANIZATION OF NEW ORLEANS:
THE LOUISIANA PURCHASE TO THE CIVIL WAR
1804-1861

1804   Blaise Cenas was appointed first postmaster of New Orleans.

March 26. The United States Congress divided the Louisiana Purchase Territory into the upper, larger portion, known as the Territory of Louisiana (north of $33°$), and the lower portion, the area that later became the state of Louisiana in 1812, called the Territory of Orleans (south of $33°$).

A legislative council, consisting of a governor and thirteen citizens appointed by the president of the United States, governed the Territory of Orleans.

June 2. James Pitot was named mayor of New Orleans.

July 27. John Mowry founded the first English language newspaper in New Orleans, the semi-weekly Louisiana Gazette with the motto "American Commerce and Freedom."

October 5. William C.C. Claiborne was inaugurated as the first governor of the Territory of Orleans.

1805   The College of Orleans, the first institution of higher learning in the city was established, but not opened until six years later.

February 22. The city of New Orleans was incorporated.

March 4. The first election to select aldermen was held.

April 19. The legislative council chartered the New Orleans Library Society as a joint stock company with an unlimited number of shares. It had the privilege of conducting a lottery.

June 16. The first Protestant church in the city was established by fifty-three protestants who chose an Episcopalian clergyman as head of Christ's Church on Canal Street.

July 27. A physician, John Watkins, was appointed mayor and a member of the territorial council by Claiborne.

December. New Orleans was fortified by General Wilkinson against Aaron Burr's expedition which Mississippi authorities broke up near Natchez.

1806   The population of New Orleans was about 12,000, of which 7,500 were white.

The council of New Orleans created a city police force to be known as the gardes de ville, eliminating the military elements of the gens d'armes.

The council also prohibited the use of shingle roofs, provided inspection of chimneys, and established rules aimed at preventing looting during fires.

The city council passed a "bucket ordinance," which required all householders to keep two buckets in readiness in case of a fire.

1808   January 30. The Theatre St. Philippe opened and soon became the center of the French world of fashion in the city.

March 9. James Mather was appointed mayor.

1810   A typographical union, one of the first in the United States, was organized in New Orleans.

The plantation of Claude Treme was purchased by the city and subdivided as the Faubourg Treme. New Orleans would now expand in all directions.

March 6. The earliest lottery law was passed by the city council.

July 4. The first celebration in honor of the signing of the Declaration of Independence took place in the Theatre St. Philippe.

1811   A meat market below St. Anne Street, begun in 1807, was destroyed in a hurricane.

April 30. The bank of New Orleans was chartered.

November 4. At a convention in New Orleans a state constitution was adopted.

1812   The City Charter of 1805 was amended; the mayor was to be elected; he was required to have been a resident of the city for four years, and to possess in his own name, for the last year in the city, real estate valued at $3,000.00 or more. Voters were required to have a minimum of $500.00 in real estate.

January 10. The first steamboat, the <u>Orleans</u>, built on one of Fulton's models by Nicholas Roosevelt, 116 feet long and 20 feet wide, arrived in New Orleans from Pittsburgh.

April 30. Louisiana was admitted to the Union as the eighteenth state, and New Orleas became the capital.

October 8. Nicholas Girod was elected mayor. He was French in culture and orientation and did not speak any English. He offered Napoleon I sanctuary in New Orleans.

December 1. General Andrew Jackson became head of the military government in New Orleans.

1813   The meat market near St. Anne Street was rebuilt.

1814   Henry M. Shreve navigated the steamboat <u>Enterprise</u> from Pittsburgh down the Ohio River into the Mississippi to New Orleans, carrying supplies to General Andrew Jackson.

December. British forces placed New Orleans under siege until January 1815.

1815   The population of the city reached 33,000.

An asylum for destitute orphan boys opened in New Orleans under the direction of Julian Poydras.

January 8. Though the Treaty of Ghent had been signed with Great Britain on December 24, 1814, General Andrew Jackson, with the aid of pirates and patriots, defeated the British in the final action at the Battle of New Orleans.

September 4. August McCarty was elected mayor, succeeding LeBreton Dorgenois who had been acting mayor since November 6, 1812.

1817   The first action was taken by the city council to limit prostitution.

A beginning was made to cover the streets in New Orleans with cobblestones.

April 15. The Louisiana Gazette, edited by John Mowry, became a triweekly and was published in both English and French.

1818

An amendment to the city charter of 1805 extended suffrage for municipal officers to all free white male citizens of the United States, aged 21 years and over, residing in the city for six months and having paid a tax to the city within the year preceding the election.

October. John Davis, an impressario of New Orleans, received a loan of $15,000.00 from the city government to complete a theater.

1819

The Old Orleans Ballroom was built by John Davis, proprietor of a gambling hall a few doors away. It became a center for New Orleans social life for the next decade.

1820

The fourth national census showed New Orleans was the fifth largest city in the United States after Boston. Population of the city was 41,000 while that of the state of Louisiana was 153,407.

An iron fence was constructed around the Place d'Armes as part of a comprehensive plan for the square submitted by Benjamin H. Latrobe.

The Physico-Medical Society was founded in New Orleans.

Imported granite blocks from Belgium were placed on Charter Street in front of the Cabildo Palace.

April 20. Joseph Roffignac, of a noble family in Angoulême, was elected mayor.

1821

Jean Jacques Audubon set up his art studio in the city.

New Orleans was lighted for the first time with lampposts set at diagonal corners of the principal streets.

Judah Touro, now a successful merchant and philanthropist, donated a building to house the first city library.

1822	Fifty constables patrolled the city by night in small squads with the right to search any "wayfarers."
	March 12. New Orleans was authorized by the city council to create a fund for expenses by way of a loan.
1823	A vegetable market was built near St. Phillippes and Barracks streets.
	Benjamin Henry Latrobe developed a steam water works to provide unfiltered river water to subscribers.
	May 8. James H. Caldwell opened the American Theater on Camp Street with Frederic Reynold's comedy The Dramatist and a farce called The Romp. The theater was the first in the city to use illuminating gas, but it was built on swampy land rendering it almost inaccessible in rainy weather.
	December 9. James Brown of New Orleans was appointed minister to France by President Monroe.
1825	April 10. General Lafayette arrived in New Orleans for a five-day visit. He was entertained on a $15,000.00 grant appropriated by the state legislature, which was used to pay for a sixty-eight foot arch in the Place d'Armes set up to honor him. The artist John James Audubon painted a portrait of the distinguished visitor.
1827	François Xavier Martin (1762-1846) published the first comprehensive History of Louisiana in New Orleans.
	Young Louisianans, who had recently returned from completing their education in Europe, celebrated the first recorded observance of Mardi Gras on Shrove Tuesday, the last day before Lent.
1828	May 12. Denis Prieur became mayor of New Orleans.
1829	April. The first volunteer fire company was organized in the city.
	May 8. Louis Moreau Gottschalk, outstanding pianist and composer, was born in New Orleans.
1830	A Captain Grant built the first railroad in the city, which ran from the Elysian Fields to Milnburg.

January 4. The seat of the Louisiana government was moved to Donaldsville. Bored by small-town life, the legislators, in the first act of the following session (1831) voted to return the capital to New Orleans.

1831

April 23. The Pontchartrain Railroad of Captain Grant was completed and offered both freight and passenber service. It was the first railroad to be built west of the Alleghenies.

October 25. The first cholera epidemic hit New Orleans; about 6,000 died in 20 days.

1833

The Congregational church was established in the city as a result of a split in the membership of the First Presbyterian church.

A Baptist church was established.

Lafayette Cemetary Number One was founded in the suburbs.

The wealthy citizens of New Orleans moved in increasing numbers to three suburbs: Lafayette, Livaudais, and Religieuse, which were united to form a "city" called Lafayette.

Thomas Banks built a three story edifice known as Banks Arcade with a glass-roofed court, that combined an auction market, barroom, and offices.

Bernard Marigny, a wealthy Creole, made the Mardi Gras a regularly celebrated event.

1834

A new parish prison was built in the Faubourg Treme, and the old prison behind the Cabildo was demolished. This prison was the center of public execution until 1883.

The Exchange Bank built the St. Charles Hotel, and the Improvement Bank built the St. Louis Hotel with a facade copied by French architects from the Rue de Rivoli in Paris.

1835

A merchants exchange building, designed by Gallier and Dakin, facing Royal and Exchange Places, was constructed.

The building of St. Patricks church for English speaking Catholics was begun.

The St. Charles Theater opened with a performance of

School for Scandal. Built at a cost of $350,000.00, it had 47 boxes and 4,000 seats; no playhouse in the United States was its equal, and few in Europe could compare to it in opulence.

The New Orleans and Carrolton Railway Company opened the city's first rail passenger service on St. Charles Avenue. The cars were pulled by horses and mules.

The first rowing club was founded in New Orleans with headquarters on the New Basin Canal.

April 2. The Medical College which eventually developed into the University of Louisiana (1847) and Tulane University (1884) was established by a group of physicians.

A serious yellow fever epidemic was reported in the city.

Summer. The New Basin Canal, begun in 1831, opened. It was dug by hand through a swamp at a cost of more than one million dollars by the American community in the city in rivalry with the Creole elements. It was six miles long, six feet deep, sixty feet wide, and competed with the Creole controlled Carondelet Canal which terminated in the lower part of the city.

1836

The Commercial Bank of New Orleans financed the first complete water and gas works.

March 8. A new charter was imposed on the city by the state legislature, resulting from frictions between Creoles and the rapidly increasing population of Anglo-Saxon origin. The city was divided into three municipalities, each with its own board of aldermen, under one mayor, and a general council composed of the three municipal councils. The Vieux Carré (French Quarter) included in the first municipality dominated by Creoles, with the old Cabildo Palace as City Hall; Faubourg St. Mary was part of the second municipality and the Faubourg Marigny part of the third.

The new charter reserved to the city the right to administer the port and to fix and collect wharfage fees.

1837

The history of organized French opera in New Orleans began at the Théâtre d'Orléans.

The official opening of the St. Charles Hotel brought universal acclaim for its architecture and comfort.

January 25. The first issue of the Picayune appeared in the city. It was founded by Col. Francis Asbury Lumsden (1806-1860) and George Wilkins Kendall (1807-1867) as a "penny press" to attract a large following.

May 13. A financial crash paralysed economic life in the city when fourteen banks suspended payment in specie. Each municipality issued its own currency.

1838   The American community of the city built the Poydras market as a supplement to the old French market.

The United States Mint was opened on a square bounded by Esplanade, Barracks, Decatur, and North Peters Streets.

Shrove Tuesday. The first Mardi Gras parade was held in New Orleans.

May 12. Charles Genois became mayor.

September 28. Henry Hobson Richardson, eminent American architect, was born in St. James Parish.

1839   The first plays in the German language were performed at the National Theater, where more than two hundred were given until the season of 1870-71.

October 1. The city deficit was over three million dollars with an annual interest of $103,000.00.

1840   New Orleans became the fourth largest city in the United States with a population of 102,193.

Antoine's Restaurant was founded by Antoine Alciatore. It was destined to become the most famous eating place in the city.

The first Presbyterian congregation was organized in the city.

A French traveler, C.C. Robin, visited New Orleans and found wide-spread indolence and corruption.

January 8. Gen. Andrew Jackson arrived in New Orleans aboard the steamer Vicksburg and presided at the laying of the cornerstone of a monument that was being constructed at the Place d'Armes, commemorating the Battle of New Orleans.

May 11. William Freret became mayor.

Summer. St. Paul's Evangelical Lutheran church was founded.

1841 The city council established New Orleans' first tax-supported free public school system with an initial budget of $105,000.00.

The Boston Club was founded in the city by a "coterie of wealthy gentlemen."

1842 The St. Charles Theatre, known in the city as the "Temple of the Drama," burned to the ground. No comparable theater was ever to be built in New Orleans to replace it.

April 4. Denis Prieur was returned to the mayorship.

1843 February 27. William Freret was elected mayor once again.

1844 The Library of the City of New Orleans opened to the public.

The New Orleans National Art Gallery of Paintings was founded.

May 13. Joseph Edgard Montegut became mayor.

May 18. A fire destroyed ten squares of the city bounded by Franklin, Canal, Common, and Claiborne streets.

1845 The city grew by 295 buildings, mostly of brick and granite, erected at the average cost of $3,500.00.

January 20. Baroness Micaela Pontalba (1795-1874), daughter of the former Spanish governor of the city Don Almonester y Roxas, obtained a permit to erect arcades on St. Peter and St. Ann streets, opposite the Place d'Armes.

May 14. The constitution of Louisiana was democratized by broadening the electoral franchise and by electing the governor by direct popular vote; free public schools were established throughout the state, and a state superintendent of education was appointed.

May 24. Sam Houston spoke in New Orleans on behalf of the Texas cause.

July. Gen. Zachary Taylor left New Orleans with 1,500 men for the Mexican campaign.

November 10. John Slidell, a prominent New Orleans citizen was appointed minister to Mexico by President Polk. He had the delicate task of adjusting difficulties between the two countries on the eve of war.

1846

New machinery for the refining of sugar, invented by Norbert Rillieux, revolutionized the industry in New Orleans.

May 11. Abdil Daily Crossman, born in Maine, became mayor of his adopted city.

The Picayune scooped the world on the Mexican War when George W. Kendall, one of the first modern war correspondents, sent his copy by pony express.

1847

The Medical College of New Orleans was renamed the University of Louisiana.

Touro Synagogue was erected, one of the most impressive structures in the city.

May 15. There was a great display of fireworks in the city, as part of a celebration in honor of victories in Mexico.

December 3-5. Gen. Zachary Taylor, the hero of the Mexican War, was welcomed to the city by an estimated crowd of 40,000 people.

1848

July 8. Louisiana veterans of the Mexican War paraded through the city and were given a huge demonstration of thanks by crowds of citizens.

August 1. Joseph Cohn founded the first German language newspaper in New Orleans, the Neue Orleanser Deutsche Zeitung.

CHRONOLOGY

1849

The Southern Yacht Club was formed, the second oldest in the United States.

The State capital moved from New Orleans to Baton Rouge.

The Varieties Theater opened with great acclaim.

The Washington and New Orleans Telegraph Company opened service in New Orleans.

The Pontalba buildings, inspired by Parisian architectural models, were completed.

February 22. The cornerstone of the Custom House, designed by A.T. Wood, was laid.

May 3. A serious flood in the city severely damaged 220 inhabited squares and drove 12,000 people from their homes.

1850

A special tax of $400,000.00 was assessed by the city council to cover the damage of the recent flood.

Gallier Hall, a new city hall for the second municipality was completed.

The name of the Place d'Armes was changed to Jackson Square.

The Mechanic's Institute was founded in the city.

A cholera epidemic that fanned out into the Middle West was reported in the city.

July 19. Pope Pius IX created the Archdiocese of New Orleans.

October 26. The New Orleans public school system was greatly enlarged from funds left to the city for that purpose by John McDonogh (1779-1850), a wealthy but miserly merchant while alive. The bequest amounted to more than $750,000.00.

1851

An important New Orleans meeting place and center for organizing the carnival, the Old Gem Saloon, was erected.

Under the management of the famous impressario P.T. Barnum, Jenny Lind, the "Swedish Nightingale," gave thirteen concerts in New Orleans, grossing $87,000.00.

August 21. Riots by Spanish inhabitants caused heavy damage to property.

1852

The Sister of Charity from Emmitsburg, Maryland, opened the Maison de Santé that became the nucleus of the hospital system of New Orleans.

February. The Southwestern Railroad Convention, meeting in New Orleans, selected this city rather than Mobile as the southern terminus of a North-South railroad that eventually became the Illinois-Central.

February 23. The state leigslature imposed a new charter upon the city that greatly extended its boundaries to include Lafayette City, densely populated with German and Irish immigrants, making it the fourth municipality. New stringent provisions controlling the funding of the city debt were also included in the charter.

June 18. An official seal for the city of New Orleans was approved by the city council. It contained thirty-one stars and showed two Indians beside three wagons over which rays of the sun were slanting; there was an alligator at the bottom and a bearded reclining figure of Neptune representing the Mississippi River.

1853

One of the most severe epidemics of yellow fever took the lives of 11,000 people in New Orleans, while the population of many towns was\totally wiped out.

The Academy of Music opened next to a reconstructed St. Charles Theatre, providing a place for circuses, minstrel shows, and burlesque throughout the century.

The New Orleans Academy of Sciences was founded.

The Bank of New Orleans was chartered.

April 7. Pierre Soulé of New Orleans (1801-1870), born in France and an outstanding lawyer and political leader, was appointed minister to Spain by President Pierce.

May 10. The city hall, designed by James Gallier, Sr., was dedicated.

1854

Public executions were officially ended; henceforth, they took place in the parish prison before a small number of witnesses.

April 1. Lexington defeated Lecomte in the Great Post State Stake at the Metarie Course in New Orleans.

April 10. John L. Leis became mayor.

1855

Volunteer fire companies were disbanded, and paid firemen were placed in charge of all fire equipment in the city.

The funding of the debt of the city reduced its obligations from $7,700,000.00 to $3,000,000.00.

April 8. The Young Men's Hebrew Literary Associates was founded.

1856

An amendment to the city charter was adopted with elaborate provisions regarding assessment and taxation.

William Makepeace Thackeray, on a lecture tour, lectured at New Orleans and praised its restaurants in his book <u>A Mississippi Bubble.</u>

June 17. Charles M. Waterman became mayor.

1857

The Pickwick Club was founded.

A city ordinance concerning "lewd and abandoned women" legalized prostitution in the city.

January 10. The Carnival, as it was to be known in the future in New Orleans, came into existence with the organization of the Mystick Krewe of Comus whose subject for their first parade came from John Milton's <u>Paradise Lost</u>. It was organized by a group of businessmen in the upstairs rooms of the Old Gem Saloon on 127 Royal Street who were destined to become the most prestigious of the sponsors of the Mardi Gras.

St. Mary's Orphan Asylum was established.

April 12. Eighty miles of the New Orleans, Opelousas, and Great Northern Railroad were completed.

1858

The first normal school in the South was established at New Orleans.

The Mardi Gras had thirty-one floats that cost $20,000.00.

A new charter for the city strengthened the power of the police.

June 3-7. The Vigilantes, a group of outraged New Orleans citizens, forced the resignation of Mayor Waterman on charges of corruption, by seizing the Cabildo Palace and holding it by force of arms. The Vigilantes were made up of Know-Nothings who rioted and terrorized foreigners in defiance of the police.

June 21. Gerard Strich was elected mayor; he immediately reformed the police force by purging about 400 men and installing modern devices like the police and fire telegraph.

December. Paul Morphy, of Creole parentage, defeated the best chess players in Europe and was declared world champion after defeating Adolf Anderson.

1859

February 26. An auction sale of the art collection of James Robb of New Orleans included important paintings by Rubens, Snyders, Vernet, and David, many of which had been brought to the city by French immigrants.

September. Four thousand Vigilantes broke up a powerful gang of cattle thieves in a suburb of the city.

December 1. The French Opera House opened at the corner of Bourbon and Toulouse streets with a performance of Rossini's _Guillaume Tell._

1860

The population of New Orleans reached 168,675 of which 40% were foreign born, with 24,000 Irish and 14,000 Germans. There were 13,000 blacks recorded as living in the city.

St. Mary's Dominican College, a Roman Catholic institution was founded as a liberal arts college for women.

June 18. John T. Monroe became mayor.

November 19. Adelina Patti made her operatic debut at the French Opera House in Donizetti's _Lucia di Lammermoor._

CHRONOLOGY 23

1861   Solari's, a famous grocery store, was established on the corner of Royal and Iberville streets.

The criminal activities of the Sicilian Mafia in New Orleans were mentioned for the first time in the newspapers of the city.

January 26. Louisiana adopted the Ordinance of Secession.

March 21. The "republic" of Louisiana joined the Confederacy.

November 8. John Slidell, now a Confederate commissioner to France, was taken from the <u>Trent</u>. This incident almost caused a war between Great Britain and the United States.

NEW ORLEANS FROM THE CIVIL WAR TO WORLD WAR I: GROWTH OF A SOUTHERN COMMERCIAL METROPOLIS 1862-1914

1862   New Orleans sent 20,000 men to the front.

January 31. The city council sold the right of way for three new railroads on which horse-cars could run through the city.

March 17. Judah P. Benjamin of New Orleans was appointed Confederate secretary of state by Jefferson Davis.

April 24-25. Flag Officer David E. Farragut, with the United States Gulf Squadron, sailed past the forts guarding New Orleans.

April 30. The city surrendered to Farragut and his Federal forces.

May 1. General Benjamin F. Butler began his controversial rule of New Orleans as a military governor. The Confederate capital was removed to Opelousas and after one session to Shreveport.

May 15. General Butler issued Order Number 28 making any woman in New Orleans liable to treatment as a prostitute if she in any way showed disrespect for the officers and men of the Union Army.

June 7. Under orders from General Butler, a New Orleans man was hanged in front of the United States Mint for having torn down the Federal flag.

May 16. John T. Monroe was officially removed as mayor of the city.

December 14. General N.P. Banks relieved General Butler as military governor of New Orleans.

1863

The <u>Daily Times</u> was founded to keep the anxious citizens informed about the war.

The first black public school in New Orleans' history was opened.

April. The Harmony Club was formed by leading Jewish citizens of the city.

1864

Railway mail service was introduced to the city.

May 11. The constitution of Louisiana was amended, abolishing slavery. A great black mass meeting was held in New Orleans to celebrate the emancipation.

1865

May 26. The last Confederate army in the field, the Trans-Mississippi, commanded by General Edmund Kirby-Smith, surrendered. Louisiana came under complete federal control, with the seat of the military government at New Orleans.

1866

Charles Gayarré (1805-1895), a grandson of New Orleans' first mayor Jean Boré, published his <u>History of Louisiana</u> in English.

A mild yellow fever epidemic took 185 lives in the city.

July. The first horse-drawn street cars were placed in operation on the St. Charles and Carondelet Railroad.

July 30. The reconvening of the state's Constitutional Convention lead to race riots in front of the Mechanics Institute, resulting in a blood-bath and the death of at least 38 (mostly black) persons. One hundred and forty-seven people were wounded.

1867

A yellow fever epidemic hit the city and took over 3,000 lives.

The Knights of the White Camelia was organized in New Orleans. Like other secret societies being founded throughout the South, it was dedicated to the cause of defending "white supremacy."

John A. Morris and Charles T. Howard formed the Louisiana State Lottery Company. They agreed to pay $40,000.00 a year to the New Orleans Charity Hospital Fund in exchange for the franchise.

March 28. Edward Heath became mayor.

1868

June 10. John R. Conway became mayor.

June 25. An act of the United States Congress readmitted Louisiana to the Union.

June 27. The Louisiana legislature met at New Orleans to ratify the Fourteenth Amendment to the Federal Constitution.

August 11. The Louisiana lottery began to function in the city.

October 20. A board of metropolitan police was formed by Act 74 of the state legislature, creating a force with five commissioners for the city.

1869

An education act passed by the state legislature placed the New Orleans school system under a board of education appointed by the State Board of Education, a measure desired by the Rev. T.W. Conway, state superintendent of education.

January 16. Seven water commissioners were named after the city bought the waterworks from the Commercial Bank of New Orleans for $2,000,000.00 payable in five percent bonds.

1870

The city population reached 191,418.

The completion of the Louisiana and Texas railroad gave the city far better access to the West and Northwest.

The yellow fever toll was 558 lives for the year.

March 16. The Republican dominated state legislature in extra session imposed a new charter upon the city vesting the municipal government in the hands of a mayor and seven administrators for finance, commerce, assessments, police, accounts, and waterworks-public buildings.

April 4. Benjamin Franklin Flanders became mayor.

June 30. The steamboats Robert E. Lee and Natchez began their historic race at New Orleans.

1871 The city purchased 280 acres of land for $800,000.00 for Upper City Park, which soon became known as Audubon Park.

1872 January. On Shrove Tuesday -- the day before Ash Wednesday and the beginning of Lent (Old English "Spring"), the Rex Society, an organization of New Orleans businessmen, paraded for the first time and became an important organizer of the Mardi Gras, along with the Knights of Momus and the Mystick Krewe of Comus. The Crown Prince of Russia, the future Alexander III, made up part of the list of distinguished guests for the many balls and other festivities. From this time on, the king of the Carnival came from the Rex Society.

November 30. Louis A. Wiltz became mayor.

1873 On Shrove Tuesday, the Comus Club put on a satire of Charles Darwin's biological notions called The Missing Link. This was the first Carnival parade that used masks and animal figures made in New Orleans rather than imported from France and marked the birth of a new industry in the city.

Train service was established between New Orleans and Chicago.

The monument to Robert E. Lee was dedicated in elaborate celebrations.

The French impressionist painter Edgar Degas visited New Orleans and painted "The Cotton Office in New Orleans" while living in the city.

1874 The suburban city of Carrolton was annexed to New Orleans.

April. The White League first appeared in New Orleans as a force attempting to unite the white population against the Republican government.

September 14. The White League forces defeated the Metropolitan Police under Gen. William Pitt Kellogg in a pitched battle at the head of Canal Street. Federal troops were called to restore order and reinstall General Kellogg as governor of the state.

November 30. Charles Leeds, a conservative industrialist active on the side of the white supremacists in the the September riots, became mayor of the city.

December. A city ordinance was passed which allowed the payment of taxes in cash and "script" in varying proportions.

1875

The Daily Democrat, a newspaper, was founded.

May 25. A German financier, D.H. Adler, suggested the premium bond plan to deal with the city debt, and it was accepted by the city council as a reform.

1876

By an act of the state legislature, the annexed city of Carrollton was made the seventh district of New Orleans.

The New Orleans Lawn Tennis Club was founded, one of the oldest clubs of this kind in the United States.

The first telephone was put into service in New Orleans by the firm of Horter and Fenner, manufacturers of saddlery and harnesses. The firm connected their salesroom to their factory with an apparatus purchased at the Philadelphia Exposition of 1876.

May 16. The city of New Orleans purchased from the Mexican Gulf Ship Canal Company all of their water concessions and rights for $30,000.00. The West End levee system was completed at the expense of the city.

December 19. Edward Pilsbury became mayor.

1877

The Daily Item, a newspaper that soon became the New Orleans Item, was founded.

April 24-27. The withdrawal of federal troops from the city marked the official end of the Reconstruction period in New Orleans.

1878

A serious yellow fever epidemic took a toll of 4,046 lives in the city whose population was 154,132.

A growing number of new Carnival clubs appeared, increasing the diversity and elaborateness of the parades, including the Independent Order of the Moon, The Phunny Phorty Phellows, and the Krewe of Proteus.

April 10. The city bought up bonds of the New Orleans Waterworks and received deed and incorporation rights at a cost of $1,250,000.00.

September. The New Orleans Waterworks was sold to private interests for $2,000,000.00.

November 18. Isaac W. Patton became mayor.

1879

The state legislature with act no. 133 established a board of liquidation to deal with the troubled state of the city's finances.

To increase revenue, the city council leased land in front of Jackson Square for $35,000.00 covering a period of fifty years, for the construction of a freight depot.

The United States Circuit Court handed down a definitive decision in the Trevique Case involving the New Orleans school system, which upheld the principle of segregation by ruling that " . . . any classification of education which provides substantially equal school facilities does not impair any right, and is not prohibited by the United States Constitution . . ."

July 10. James B. Eads' company of engineers, in spite of opposition from the United States Corps of Engineers, completed a jetty system that opened the port of New Orleans to new large steamships by gaining a constant depth of thirty feet of water. A great amount of money and time involved in transfer of freight at sea was saved.

1880

The newspaper The Daily States was founded in New Orleans.

Laws against cruelty to animals were promulgated by the city council, thereby ending the popular pastime and gambling activity of cock-fighting.

An art union was formed in the city to further art and culture.

The state legislature restored Baton Rouge as the state capital after it had been moved to New Orleans during the Civil War. In 1862 it had been shifted to Opalousas, thence to Shreveport, and in 1864 to New Orleans.

The United States Census revealed that the population of New Orleans was 216,090 persons, of which 57,723 were "colored." There were 566.2 miles of streets in the city, of which 472.34 were paved; the street railroad had 140 miles of single track with 313 cars pulled by some 1,641 mules with 671 men employed; the fare was five cents at all times.

The census placed the total valuation of property in the city at $91,794,350.00 or $425.00 per capita, while the net indebtedness of the city was $736,589.00 or $82.00 per capita.

The first statewide poor law was enacted in Louisiana.

New Orleans was lighted by gas provided by a private company which also maintained 3,600 street lights at a cost of $13.18 each per annum.

April. Gen. Ulysses S. Grant visited New Orleans.

December 16. Joseph A. Shakespeare became mayor.

1881

The Times-Democrat was founded when the Daily Times and Daily Democrat merged.

New Orleans was linked to the Pacific Coast by a connection with the Southern Pacific Railroad.

The total assessment of the city was $97,340,605.00 while debts were $24,000,000.00

June. An almshouse in the city, financed by funds collected from gambling houses, was established.

August 10. Committees of New Orleans citizens organized vigilante and safety committees to deal with crime, compel authorities to do their duty, see that the city spent its revenue economically, prevent abuses of the pardoning power, watch the city government, and especially to ferret out unworthy public servants and to see that they were punished.

1882

May-June. Increased power of the state legislature over the

city was achieved by the imposition of a new charter for New Orleans directed at financial reform of the city's revenue. The elected officers included the mayor, treasurer, comptroller, commissioner of public works, and a commissioner of police and public buildings. The council was made up of thirty elected members.

November 20. W.J. Behan became mayor.

1883

Zenith of the popular pleasure resort was the Spanish Fort, which had a famous casino and theater where notable events like the lectures of Oscar Wilde were presented to large audiences.

Passenger train service was established between New Orleans and California.

January 20. Women replaced men as telephone operators on the lines of the Great Southern Telephone and Telegraph Company.

1884

Paul Tulane, a wealthy New Orleans merchant, deeded real estate worth half a million dollars to the University of Louisiana, which was renamed in his honor.

Royal Street was permanently lighted by electricity.

February 22. The sixteen and a half foot statue of Robert E. Lee was unveiled atop a sixty-foot Doric column at Lee Circle.

April 29. J. Valsin Guillotte became mayor.

December 16. The World's Exposition and Cotton Centennial opened on a 249 acre tract in uptown New Orleans when the president of the United States telegraphed a signal that activated machinery in various displays. Philadephia sent its Liberty Bell to mark the occasion. The Fair was not a financial success, and the improved land used by the exposition was transformed into Audubon Park.

1885

May. The Citizens' Committee of One Hundred was created in the city to deal with abuses in municipal government.

December. A grand jury found that the city's affairs were dominated by "ring rule," the police were inefficient and "effete," and that hoodlums and burglars were allowed free-run in the city.

1886 The New Orleans Sanitarium opened as a training school for nurses, the first in the South. This sanitarium was soon to be joined with the Presbyterian Hospital.

Josephine Le Monnier Newcomb of New Orleans donated $100,000.00 to found a college for women that became Newcomb College for Women. In 1901, the Newcomb estate provided $2,668,387.00 in endowment for this college, making it one of the best endowed women's institutions in the country.

January. The entire central city was lit by electricity.

November. The Law and Order League was organized, appealing to "all parties and classes" to help combat corruption and incompetence in municipal government.

1887 February. The results of the grand jury investigation brought to an end the Shakespeare Plan for the collection of monies from gambling houses to support the Almshouse when large-scale official corruption in this process was revealed.

1888 April 24. In spite of his influence in connection with the scandals, Joseph A. Shakespeare was again elected mayor.

1889 The last mention was made in the New Orleans press of a duel. The participants were arrested by the police.

The Edison Company cooperated with a Carnival club, the Knights of Electra, to design a float for the Mardi Gras featuring an incadescent lamp using a steam generator drawn by sixteen mules.

1890 The lottery business accounted for about 45 percent of the receipts of the New Orleans Post Office.

The Italian community of the city numbered about 15,000.

March 14. Louisiana became one of the first states to legalize prize fighting. The city ordinance stipulated that no liquor was to be served at the contests, that none be held on Sundays, that the clubs donate $50.00 to charity, and that at $500.00 bond be posted before each fight.

October 15. David C. Hennessy, a popular chief of police, was murdered by a group of gangsters near his home.

1891

The <u>New Orleans Picayune</u>, under the direction of the widow of the founder, Eliza Jane Portevent, had the largest circulation in the city.

A bicycle school was set up in the city by Bert Spring.

April 25. The city council passed Ordinance 5256 which provided legislation on the reconstruction of the wharf system of the city.

March 14. Eleven Italian prisoners, alleged slayers of Chief of Police Hennessy, were taken from the parish prison and lynched.

August 11-12. After failing in two other attempts, Gen. Narcisco Lopez lead an expedition of Spanish refugees and Americans from New Orleans to Cuba in an attempt to foment a Cuban revolution against Spain.

August 21. Riots occurred in the city when news arrived about the capture of the Lopez contingent and summary executions of some of their number. The Spanish consulate in the city was demolished by the protestors.

September 1. The United States Congress agreed to pay for the damages to the Spanish consulate, though it was confirmed that General Lopez had been executed and that seventy-five Americans had been sent to Spain to stand trial.

1892

The New Orleans city library was formed by the consolidation of the Fisk Free and Public libraries of the city.

A standard numbering system was applied to all buildings in the city.

April 12. Italy accepted $25,000.00 indemnity in the matter of the New Orleans lynchings, and diplomatic relations were restored.

April 25. A leading sports authority, John Fitzpatrick, was elected mayor of New Orleans, opening up a period of widespread tension over alleged corruption in the city government. Attempts by various citizens' committees to impeach him failed.

September 7. James J. Corbett knocked out John L. Sullivan in twenty-one rounds in a New Orleans contest under the sponsorship of the Olympic Athletic Club.

1893   February. Electricity was used to drive streetcars in New Orleans.

March 20. James Biddle Eustis of New Orleans was appointed minister to France by President Cleveland.

April 6. Andy Bowen and Jack Burke battled seven hours and nineteen minutes in a 110 round draw at New Orleans in the longest bout in the history of prize fighting.

1895   The Louisiana Lottery was outlawed; the lottery moved to Honduras.

Elves of Oberon, a Carnival society was formed.

1896   O. Henry (William Sidney Porter, 1862-1910) arrived in New Orleans to continue his literary career.

The city council adopted a code of traffic regulations for bicycles requiring "wheelmen to carry lanterns after dark, to keep a hand on the wheelbars, to stay on the right side of the street, to abjure riding on the sidewalk, and to go no more than 10 miles an hour in town."

January 11. The Citizen's League of New Orleans backed lawyer-businessman Walter C. Flower for mayor; he had been president of the Cotton Exchange in 1891 and 1892.

April 24. The board of commissioners of the Port of New Orleans was given the responsibility to regulate all questions relating to the Port of New Orleans and to issue annual reports.

April 27. Walter C. Flower became mayor; he pushed through an important new city charter.

1897   The United Fruit Company opened the first wireless station in New Orleans.

Alderman Sidney Story, who had made a careful study of prostitution and its regulation in Europe, fashioned a new ordinance restricting the traffic to a specific area in the city that became known as Storyville. It was just outside the Vieux Carré within an area bounded by Iberville, Robertson, St. Louis, and Basin Streets. Sidney Story was a pseudonym for Mrs. Mary Hayden Green (1825-1908).

September 4. A serious epidemic of fever took more than 6,000 lives.

December 15. The city council decreed by Ordinance 13,838 that all electrical wires in the city be put underground.

1898   There were about 800 saloons in the city.

Klaw and Erlanger, a well-known New York theatrical booking agency, opened two theaters in New Orleans, the Crescent, with a seating capacity of 1,800 and the Tulane, with a capacity of 1,400.

1899   Enrollment in the schools of New Orleans reached 23,668, of which 20,259 were white.

The Sewage and Water Board issued a twelve million dollar bond issue.

February 28. The private street railroads, including the New Orleans and Carrollton, chartered in 1833, merged into the City Railroad Company.

1900   A police telephone system and fire alarm systems were installed in the city.

April 17. Paul Capdeville, a lawyer and businessman was elected mayor by defeating the candidate of the Citizens-League.

July 23. The Charles Race Riots broke out when a policeman named Mora attempted to arrest a black named Robert Charles, who was suspected of being an agent for Bishop Turner. Turner was head of a movement dedicated to leading blacks to new lives in Liberia.

1901   May 2. William McKinley visited New Orleans, the first president to do so while in office.

1902   Streetcar workers of New Orleans went on strike, paralyzing the city.

October 8. Strike-breakers, imported from St. Louis, attempted to run four cars on Canal Street under police protection.

October 9. The state militia entered New Orleans. The following day, the governor of Louisiana negotiated a successful compromise, which guaranteed all strikers the right to return to their jobs.

October 10. New Orleans streetcar men returned to work after their unsuccessful strike to achieve an eight hour day and twenty-five cents per hour minimum wage, in spite of public support for their cause.

1904   Loyala Academy, a fore-runner of Loyola University, was founded.

The population of New Orleans reached 300,000.

December. W. Covington Hall, the first Socialist to run in a city election in New Orleans, received 179 votes.

December 5. Martin Behrman, supported by the state machine, was elected mayor.

1905   The city council promulgated an order that allowed the demolition of an entire square of old buildings to build the Civil Courts Building on Royal Street.

The last severe outbreak of yellow fever in New Orleans occurred due to the lax enforcement of procedures in treating the breeding places of the Stegomgia mosquito in New Orleans.

Galatoire's Restaurant at 209 Bourbon Street, with a décor as simple as the food was elegant, was opened to the public.

October 18. President Theodore Roosevelt was given a cheering welcome when he appeared at City Hall during a nine hour visit.

1906   The New Orleans Symphony Society was founded; six years later, the Society was taken over by its women members.

1907   June 4. Federal intervention ended a century of lottery activity in New Orleans.

1908	The New Orleans Sewage and Water Board began an eight million dollar bond campaign.

A gift from Andrew Carnegie of $250,000.00 made possible the opening of a new city library building. |
| 1909 | Ralph de Palma set an automobile speed record, averaging sixty miles per hour for fifty miles at New Orleans.

October 30. President William Howard Taft visited New Orleans with 117 senators and congressmen, 24 governors, and 3 diplomats, to inspect the possibilities of improving the adjacent waterways. |
| 1910 | The first moving picture theater opened in New Orleans.

December 24. An international aviation tournament was held in New Orleans, where a record for a mile in a class contest was set at fifty-seven seconds. |
| 1911 | The Isaac Delgado Museum of Art in City Park, based on a gift from the New Orleans philanthropist of the same name, opened.

Loyola University, evolving from Loyola Academy, was established by the Jesuits. |
| 1912 | George Mestach, carrying mail by airplane from New Orleans to Baton Rouge, successfully completed the second such venture in air mail delivery in the United States.

The West End Sea Wall was completed at a cost of $68,255.00.

August 28. The state legislature issued a new charter for the city which was based upon the "commission plan." The city was to be governed by a mayor and four commission councilmen who constituted a commission council replacing the city council. |
| 1914 | The Times-Picayune was founded, based on a merger of the Picayune and the Times-Democrat.

The last performance was given at the French Opera House on the corner of Bourbon and Toulouse streets; the building was destroyed by fire in 1919. |

The Southern University of New Orleans moved to Scotlandville, Louisiana after having been in the city for forty years.

NEW ORLEANS BETWEEN TWO WARS: DEVELOPMENT OF A SOUTHERN REGIONAL CENTER 1915-1945

1915   New Orleans musicians introduced jazz to Chicago.

A new system of street lighting was completed with three or more lights per block.

There were 22,187 city subscribers to the Cumberland Telephone and Telegraph Company with seven exchanges.

September 29. A tropical hurricane hit the city, inflicting more than thirteen million dollars in property damage and a few fatalities.

1916   The St. Louis Hotel was demolished by real estate interests.

June 3. A "preparedness" parade was held through the center of the city with more than 40,000 marchers.

Summer. Xavier University, a Roman Catholic institution, was founded in a high school established two years earlier in the city. It had been planned originally for blacks and Indians.

1917   July 10. Storyville, infamous center of New Orleans prostitution and underworld activities, was closed by a city ordinance passed at the urging of the secretary of the navy.

1918   William Ratcliffe Irby, a New Orleans philanthropist, provided the funds for the restoration of the greatly deteriorated St. Louis Cathedral.

The old Banque de la Louisiane building was converted into a restaurant.

1919   Le Petit Theatre du Vieux Carré was organized.

A new water system was completed. It serviced more than 5,000 hydrants over 600 miles of streets, and greatly aided the 463 uniformed firemen of the city in dealing with fires.

December 2-4. The French Opera House, which had been purchased and presented to Tulane University three years earlier by an unknown donor, was destroyed by fire. Besides the loss of the building, an important musical collection was also lost.

1920

November 19. Senator Warren Harding addressed the New Orleans Association of Commerce.

December 6. Andrew J. McShane was elected mayor, replacing the Behrman machine which had controlled the city for sixteen years.

1921

The new club house of the Southern Yacht Club opened at West End.

Surrounding swampy areas were filled to make way for the demand for new housing in the wake of World War I.

The New Orleans Double Dealer was founded as a "little" literary magazine. It printed the early works of William Faulkner, Ernest Hemingway, and Thornton Wilder, among others.

May 3. The New Orleans Canal was dedicated and opened to traffic.

1922

October 3-7. An American flag, embroidered by American girls was presented in a ceremony at City Hall to the French consul and other dignitaries while a French flag was given to the city in exchange.

1923

April 1. The Parker Inner Harbor Port Development Project, a twenty year undertaking, was completed.

July 17. A city planning and zoning board was appointed.

1924

December 18. An outbreak of Boubonic Plague in New Orleans lead to an urgent request for federal aid from Congress.

1925

May 4. Martin Behrman was once again elected mayor.

September 27. Plans for a skyscraper in the business center of New Orleans were announced by financial backers of the project.

1926	New Orleans and Baltimore ports tied for second place in commercial activity.

January 12. Arthur J. O'Keefe was elected mayor.

February 21. A widespread outcry against the demolition of buildings in the Vieux Carré was sounded in the New Orleans media.

March 25. Tulane University celebrated its ninetieth year by the establishment of a chair in journalism.

June 21. The New Orleans Cotton Exchange voted to include Houston and Galveston as delivery points for cotton.

September 22. More than 2,000 acres of marginal land adjacent to the city were improved to meet the demand for housing. |
| 1927 | April 29. Flooding forced the city engineers to blast the levee at Poydas Street, but more than $5,000,000.00 in damage occured in the parishes of St. Bernard and Plaquemines.

May 22. The United States Supreme Court invalidated zoning ordinances in the city that barred blacks.

August 14. The New Orleans police began an intensive crackdown on gambling activities in the city.

October 4. Direct shipping service, on a regular basis, began from Port New Orleans to Mexico and Columbia.

October 18. The commission council approved the first major street plan, in principle, opening the way for further operation of the docks as a municipal activity. |
| 1928 | The first bridge across Lake Pontchartrain, which is 25,000 feet long, was completed and opened to the public.

January 25. New Orleans Port Bonds were made legal investments at New York State banks. |
| 1929 | May 12. Influential organizations in the city began agitation for a city management municipal government instead of the existing commission form. |

	May 16. An attempt to impeach state Governor Huey P. Long was defeated by a bloc of fifteen senators.
	June 15. T. Semmes Walmsley became acting mayor due to the ill health of Arthur J. O'Keefe. He was known as a bitter opponent of the Huey P. Long machine.
1930	Governor Huey P. Long began to destroy the power of the New Orleans politicians who controlled gambling and prostitution in the North Rampart and Basin Street district, forcing these activities to move to the Jefferson Parish, a fifteen minute ride from Canal Street.
	Mayor Walmsley called an emergency conference of city labor leaders and businessmen to find ways to deal with the serious growth of unemployment.
	April 9. T. Semmes Walmsley was elected mayor on the democratic ticket.
	June 29. The City Auditorium opened and was dedicated to the memory of the World War I dead of the city.
	December 4. The New Orleans Public Belt Railroad got ICC permission to build a bridge over the Mississippi.
1931	April 8. Mayor T. Semmes Walmsley was indicted on a charge of investing city trust funds and failure to insure the proper audit of public funds.
1932	January 17. Demolitions in the Vieux Carré were halted by a court order.
	February 5. Momus, King of Joy, opened the Mardi Gras festivities.
	May 29. New Orleans police dispersed a group of 450 veterans demanding employment; though a shot was fired, a riot was averted.
	July 10. The city's commission council voted to preserve dueling oaks and suicide grounds as historical monuments.
1933	The <u>Times Picayune</u> purchased the <u>Daily States</u> as an afternoon and Sunday newspaper.

Five New Orleans banks failed along with many building and loan associations.

March 1. The Mardi Gras parades were cancelled because of rain.

April 13. The three breweries of New Orleans distributed one-half million gallons of beer to celebrate the end of Prohibition.

September 14. United States Senator Huey P. Long broke with the New Orleans Democratic organization.

December 21. Mayor T. Semmes Walmsley refused to accept Senator Long's candidate for district attorney.

1934 The New Orleans Federal Relief roster indicated that 11 percent of the population were receiving relief.

January 1. The first Sugar Bowl football game was played by the teams of Tulane and Temple Universities.

January 25. T. Semmes Walmsley won election as mayor, defeating the entire slate fielded by the Long machine.

January 28. Mayor Walmsley brought court action to investigate the state offices in the city controlled by Senator Long, while Senator Long brought action to investigate City Hall.

April 1. Mrs. L.S. Jessen, a Socialist who had been arrested and imprisoned in the city for distributing handbills without a permit, was released.

August. An experimental barge-tow, transporting 1,400 tons of steel from New Orleans to Houston through the Intracoastal Waterway, successfully completed the run.

August 16. The state legislature, heavily influenced by the Long machine, voted to investigate the Walmsley administration.

September. A vice squad was organized when state officials conducted hearings in the city on alleged corruption.

September 1. The governor of Louisiana, strongly influenced by Senator Long, imposed martial law on the city.

September 1. Senator Long and the Legislative Investigative Commission arrived in New Orleans.

September 5. Using radio, Senator Long employed his magnetic speech-making power to heighten the importance of the investigation.

September 6. There were reports of the firing of guns at Senator Long's home.

September 8. Newspapers in New Orleans were forced to end the printing of racing data under a law sponsored by Senator Long.

November 17. Senator Long was able to get control of the fire and police departments of New Orleans through civil service commission influence on the state level.

1935

February 24. Plans were completed for the preservation of an old landmark, the French Market.

September. Dillard University, a merger of several colleges for blacks maintained in New Orleans under Protestant auspices since the Civil War, opened its doors.

September 8. Huey P. Long was assassinated in the state capital at Baton Rouge.

December 13. The Bonnet Carré Spillway was dedicated.

December 16. The Huey P. Long Bridge across the Mississippi, five miles above the city, was opened to traffic.

1936

An amendment was added to the state constitution, which provided for the preservation and protection of historical buildings and sections of cities, and a commission was set up to look after the future of the Vieux Carré.

January 24. The New Orleans Port Commission and the Eastern Railroad struggled over the allocation of export freight.

June 26. Mayor Walmsley resigned.

August 17. Robert S. Maestri, endorsed by the Huey P. Long Democratic Committee, was elected mayor. For the

	next decade he was closely associated with the New Deal in New Orleans.
1937	Mayor Maestri introduced a system of central purchasing that reduced the city payroll by eliminating eighteen city employees of that department.

The Bonnet Carré Spillway was used for the first time when high water threatened the city.

The <u>Delgado Flash,</u> an airplane built by students of the Delgado Trades School of New Orleans, broke the world speed record for planes of that class.

March 27. An extensive cleaning program was undertaken in the Vieux Carré.

April 29. President Franklin Delano Roosevelt visited New Orleans to dedicate a mall in City Park.

December 19. A house, reportedly planned as a refuge for Napoleon Bonaparte, was restored in the Vieux Carré.

1938 October 11. Due to trading irregularities, the stocks of the New Orleans, Texas, and Mexico Railroad were stricken from the legal list of negotiable companies by the Securities Exchange Commission.

1939 A new charity hospital opened in the city.

August 22-23. A federal grand jury indicted high ranking New Orleans officials appointed by Huey P. Long for mail fraud.

1940 February 25. Federal government officials asked for New Orleans election data and summoned the grand jury to reconvene and deal with voting irregularities.

May 25. The United States Circuit Court affirmed the conviction of leading New Orleans political figures in mail fraud.

August 7. The New Orleans district attorney indicted high-ranking New Orleans officials for bribery.

October 22. The United States Supreme Court refused to review mail fraud indictment cases against Long appointees.

1941	Mardi Gras festivities were cancelled because of World War II.

January 19. The United States Court of Appeals upheld the convictions of those involved in a levee refunding scheme.

April 8. The State of Louisiana sued New Orleans Mayor R.S. Maestri for funds allegedly collected from the Canal Oil Company while he was the state conservation commissioner from 1929 to 1936.

May 13. The United States Supreme Court refused to review cases of those involved in the New Orleans levee refunding deal.

May 30. The editors of the <u>New Orleans States</u> and the <u>Times-Picayune</u> were fined for criticizing Mayor Maestri in connection with his indictment for fraud.

June 28. The <u>New Orleans Item</u> discontinued its Sunday edition and increased the price of its daily. |
| 1942 | January 28. Mayor Maestri was reelected along with the entire Democratic ticket.

May. The Delta Shipyards in New Orleans completed the first 10,500 ton ship called the <u>William C.C. Claiborne</u>. |
| 1944 | May 5. A new musical director and permanent conductor, M. Freccia, was appointed by the New Orleans Symphony Orchestra.

October 27. The United States cruiser <u>New Orleans</u> was damaged twice in action. |

NEW ORLEANS SINCE WORLD WAR II:
A HISTORICAL CITY IN CONTEMPORARY AMERICA
1945-1970

1945	By an ordinance passed by the city council, the boundaries of the Vieux Carré, as described in the Charter of 1936, were reduced. Many buildings in the fringe areas of the oldest parts of the city were demolished until this ordinance was declared unconstitutional.

May 8. Adolf Hitler was hanged in effigy as part of the Victory in Europe Day in the city. |

August 8. Mayoralty candidate S. Wimberly urged women to vote in order to implement municipal reform.

September. New Orleans police were accused of supporting an "illegal" lock-out of workers at the H.G. Hill Stores which were involved in a bitter dispute with various unions.

1946

January 23. The old regular Democratic machine was defeated by the reform ticket of LeLasseps S. Morrison, who was elected mayor in a landslide. He immediately began a tremendous physical rehabilitation of the city.

February 17. The Home Development Committee of the New Orleans Association of Commerce urged various interests to invest more money for veterans' housing in the city.

April 21. The New Orleans municipal employees associations, threatened by a cost conscious new administration, demanded civil service status.

September 1. Reports circulated that the city's professional gamblers were consolidating their efforts behind the deposed old regular Democratic political clubs.

October 27 - November 3. New Orleans garbage collectors and incinerator workers went on strike. Mayor Morrison and businessmen collected garbage to affirm the "proper" civic spirit, and the United States Navy allowed its personnel to volunteer and aid the improvised garbage collection force.

1947

March 2. A new opera house building was under construction.

March 15. Irate real estate interests and property owners petitioned the New Orleans district attorney for the impeachment of Mayor Morrison. The group (including the mayor's father-in-law) alleged improper use of permit and contingent funds.

March 19. The move to impeach the mayor failed and the petition was withdrawn.

June 13. City officials made their opposition to the St. Lawrence Seaway Project known.

June 15. The municipal government approved city improvement projects estimated to cost forty-one million dollars.

August 3. The New Orleans Port Authority began an extensive publicity program on industrial and tourist facilities in the city.

November 25. The city government sought a permit from the ICC to build a railroad terminal financed by a bond issue.

1948

February 22. Tulane University sponsored a seminar on public administration designed for high-level government officials.

April 29. Having received an ICC permit, the city offered a bond issue for the building of the Union Railroad Terminal at fifteen million dollars.

June 3. Various political groups from the city protested in front of the state capital building demanding greater autonomy for the city.

July 7. A bill signed by the governor of Louisiana, making Saturdays a legal holiday, was the subject of wide-spread protest in the city.

July 7. A fifteen million dollar issue sale was temporarily halted by bankers because of legal difficulties.

December 7. A conference on tropical medicine was held in the city.

1949

February 8. A special tax levied upon visiting tugboats and barges by the Port of New Orleans was upheld by the United States Supreme Court.

March 21. Mayor Morrison promoted a city plan aimed at increasing trade connections with Latin American countries and the city.

September 22. Increasing evidence submitted to the media indicated that racketeers were planning to seize control of the city's political life after the ouster of Mayor Morrison.

December 18. Two New Orleans policemen were dismissed

after charges had been submitted against them indicating that they had abused citizens of the city and "abridged their civil rights."

1950

The population of New Orleans was 570,445. It was the fifth largest city in the United States.

The state legislature restored the mayor-council system of government to the city, increasing the number of commissioners to seven, each elected by a separate district.

January 22. The white supremacist candidate for mayor, A.A. Cobb, along with a sympathetic crowd, demonstrated in the city against Mayor Morrison's gift of the "keys to the city" to a black, Dr. Ralph J. Bunche.

January 23. The New Orleans clergy made a unified plea to the city's voters to reject bigotry when casting their votes in the mayoral election.

January 25. Mayor Morrison was reelected with a record black vote supporting him. He defeated C.C. Zatarain.

May 12. Cardinal Spellman and six other distinguished American clergymen were made honorable citizens of the city by the city council.

June 6. The _New Orleans Item_ published evidence of political corruption, which instigated a probe by a committee of the United States Senate.

1951

A serious blaze destroyed valuable costumes and floats of the carnival club "Rex." The Korean War also interfered with the full celebration of the Mardi Gras in the city.

March 6. The Protestant clergy of the city protested the erection of a statue of St. Francis Xavier on city property. They claimed it was in violation of the separation of church and state principle and brought a suit against Mayor Morrison.

March 22. Judge Yarrut of the United States Circuit Court dismissed the St. Francis Xavier statue suit brought against the mayor by the Protestant clergy of the city.

November 27. The FCC forgave New Orleans radio station

WDSU for refusing radio time to the white supremacist candiate A.A. Cobb.

1952

January 28. New Orleans gamblers and officials, who figured in the Senate Crime Committee probe, accepted an invitation to bid for Senator Estes Kefauver's coonskin cap to aid the March of Dimes drive.

February 21. Supporters of reelected Sheriff H. Reid, whom newsmen accused of being involved in gambling activities in the city, shouted and threw copies of newspapers into the Press Building.

March 27. The New Orleans Times-Picayune, States, and Item dropped racing news at Police Superintendant Scheuring's request; the Sports Bulletin, which was widely distributed in the city, still carried the data.

May 8. A federal grand jury scored the New Orleans police for permitting wide-open gambling in St. Bernard and West Baton Rouge Parishes.

December 14. New Orleans planned its sesquicentennial celebration of the Louisiana Purchase.

1953

A police department scandal broke open, due to the probe by former FBI official Aaron M. Kohn, which had been requested by prominent New Orleans citizens. The result was a complete shake-up of the department and upgrading of requirements for police work.

January 5. Widespread industrial diversification by the New Orleans business community was reported in the news media.

April 19. New Orleans newspaper reporters were acquitted on charges of defaming public officials and gamblers in the city.

October 11. The New Orleans Sesquicentennial Celebration of the Louisiana Purchase featured exhibits of important French art and historical documents.

December 13. Mayor Morrison received the LaGuardia Award for outstanding achievement in municipal affairs.

1954	April 7. Mayor DeLesseps S. Morrison was reelected for the fourth time.

May 1. The ninth city charter since 1805 was approved by the city council.

May 2. The New Orleans Union Passenger Terminal was dedicated. Built at a cost of sixteen million dollars, it provided facilities for eight railroads, replaced five depots, and was part of a fifty-seven million dollar public improvement program. It represented the first such facility in the United States to be wholly publicly owned.

December 24. Basin Street, one of the most important tourist attractions in the city, was widened and "improved." |
| 1955 | Work began in the city on a new civic center.

March 1. The Inter-American Investment Conference was held in the city. |
| 1956 | February 16. Heavy rains flooded parts of the city causing some fatalities and about $250,000 in damaged property. The debris from the Mardi Gras celebration clogged water mains.

March 29. President Dwight D. Eisenhower signed a bill authorizing the construction of a new seaway for the port of New Orleans.

May 22. William Zeckendorf reported that his real estate firm, Webb and Knapp, planned to develop the mineral resources of 35,000 acres of land in the New Orleans vicinity which had been acquired from Godchaux Sugars, Inc. |
| 1957 | A twenty-four mile long bridge across Lake Pontchartrain was put into operation.

March 1. New Orleans blacks boycotted the Mardi Gras as a form of protest against segregation in the city.

March 9. A new telephone fire alarm system was activated; it contained 750 alarm boxes which were installed and maintained by the telephone company.

May 7. The new city hall and civic center was dedicated. |

November 24. A statue of Simon Bolivar, a gift of Venezuela, was accepted and dedicated by the city.

December. Congressman Edward Hebert was present to dedicate the century-old project of the Mississippi River-Gulf Outlet, completed at an estimated cost of ninety-six million dollars.

1958

Louisiana State University in New Orleans, an integral part of the state university in Baton Rouge, was established.

February 5. Mayor DeLesseps S. Morrison was reelected for the sixth time.

February 6. The city of New Orleans sold 2.2 million dollars worth of Street Improvement Bonds at 3.255 percent interest, 2 million dollars worth of Aviation Bonds at 3.254 percent interest, and 1.2 million dollars worth of Sewer Bonds at 3.248 percent interest.

February 16. Tulane University set up an adult education unit to study the city and its problems.

May 31. All signs reading "for colored patrons only" were removed from the transit vehicles of the city.

July 15. The United States Justice Department approved the terms of sale of the New Orleans Item to the Times-Picayune Publishing Company for 3.4 million dollars. The Item was to be combined with the New Orleans States.

October 17. The United States Appeals Court affirmed the grant by the FCC of television Channel 4 to Loyola University, ruling that the University, though Jesuit, was legally and financially autonomous from the Society of Jesus. The suit had been filed by Protestant groups in the city.

1959

January 8. International House, a privately supported New Orleans agency, which fostered trade for the Port of New Orleans, reported that the port was the second busiest in the United States, moving from sixteenth place in 1939.

July 16. Judge J. Skelly Wright of the United States Circuit Court ordered the New Orleans School Board to submit a desegregation plan by March 1960, and urged the public to cooperate in its formulation.

November 1. The New Orleans Stock Exchange was consolidated with the Mid-West Stock Exchange, and its members transferred to Chicago.

1960

Only 2.3 percent of the population was foreign born, of which the majority was Italian.

Use of the Tidewater Ship Channel cut forty miles off the route from New Orleans to the Gulf of Mexico.

January 8. Mayor Morrison learned at a trial linking him to the Communist Party that his private secretary had joined an organization listed by the House Un-American Activities Committee as a communist front.

January 13. Complaints of unlawful arrest lodged against the New Orleans Police Department by Swedish Merchant Marine officers led to complicated negotiations between the Swedish foreign office and the city council.

April 6. A private school plan was presented by some groups in New Orleans to thwart integration; segregationists promised financial aid to build new private school units, hoping to receive some state tax money.

April 30. An award was presented to French President DeGaulle, and a street in the city was named after him.

May 31. The publisher S. I. Newhouse attempted to add the two newspapers of the city to his chain of fifteen.

August 18. Louisiana's Governor Davis ordered state officials to take legal control of the state schools in order to prevent integration.

November 5. The state legislature passed a bill to abolish school boards in the state of Louisiana as part of a package of legislation to block black racial integration in schools.

November 14. A ruling by the United States Supreme Court forced the integration of the public schools of the city but protest continued when five black girls were admitted into the William Franz and McDonogh No. 19 Elementary School, protected by U.S. marshalls.

November 16. Armed clashes occurred between police and

citizens of the city over integration, and the five black girls attended the elementary school almost alone until December.

November 28. The media reported a serious decline of business in the city due to the integration dispute.

December 6. Mayor Morrison urged a moratorium on further news coverage of the integration dispute, arguing such coverage gave the erroneous impression that the city was filled with violence.

December 13. The United States Supreme Court unanimously denied Louisiana's application for a stay on the desegregation of schools in New Orleans.

1961

January 13. The state legislature voted to remove the superintendant of schools of New Orleans because of his moderate position on integration.

June 4. New Orleans East, a fifty square mile tract within the city limits, was the largest metropolitan development area in the United States under single ownership.

June 14. Mayor Morrison resigned his post and accepted the appointment as U.S. ambassador to the Organization of American States.

June 21. Councilman Victor Schiro was named acting mayor. He continued the extensive building program that was started by Mayor Morrison's administration. A network of expressways and interstate highways was in the process of transforming the access to the city in all directions.

September 1. Crime Commission Director Kohn alleged that racketeers and brothel owners contributed to the 1946 mayoralty campaign of former Mayor Morrison. Ambassador Morrison denied all these allegations.

September 8. The second year of desegregation of the New Orleans school system started without incident, but local authorities still failed to comply, and Archbishop Joseph F. Rummel allowed Catholic parochial schools to remain segregated at the beginning of the 1961-62 term.

1962

March 27-28. Archbishop Joseph F. Rummel ordered all Catholic schools in the Diocese of New Orleans to be integrated. He enforced his order by the excommunication of three Catholic citizens who attempted to oppose his order a few weeks later.

April 4. Acting Mayor Victor Schiro was elected mayor in a Democratic victory in the city election.

May 4. President John F. Kennedy visited New Orleans unexpectedly to give an address at the dedication of the new Nashville Avenue Wharf.

June 5. The media syndicate of S.I. Newhouse finally gained control over the opposition of stockholders and purchased the Times-Picayune Publishing Company.

August 4. City leaders signaled the importance to the economy of New Orleans of the United States rivalry with the Soviet Union in the space program, urging business leaders to be aware of its implications.

September 5. Roman Catholic schools in New Orleans admitted blacks for the first time without incident; the change involved about thirty schools and one hundred and fifty black pupils.

1963

July 13. The slow progress of black integration in the New Orleans schools was blamed by newsmen on the restraint of the blacks themselves.

August 16. The United States Court of Appeals ruled that a New Orleans bank could not establish a branch by merely creating a holding company to control that bank.

December 11. The managing editor of the New Orleans Times-Picayune and the States-Item died.

1964

March 6. The Hilton Hotel chain decided to build a twelve million dollar hotel in the Vieux Carré to open in 1966.

September 27. The price of the Times-Picayune rose from five cents to ten cents.

1965

January 11. Twenty-one black football players boycotted an AFL All-Star game because of continued patterns of segretation in that city.

February 11. Mrs. B.J. Gaillot, excommunicated for defying Roman Catholic desegregation policies in the city in 1962, wired the Pope at the Vatican for permission to make a public confession.

August 14. The Louisiana Power and Light Company announced that its new headquarters in New Orleans would be a windowless, aluminum-sheathed skyscraper.

September. Hurricane Betsy was responsible for widespread flooding in the city and some loss of life.

November 7. Mayor Victor Schiro was reelected when an official recount showed that he won by 514 votes.

1966

January 6. The Ford Foundation gave a grant to the New Orleans school system.

January 12. The United States Department of Justice sued the St. James Parish school district in New Orleans for filing an "unacceptable" desegregation plan.

January 20. The New Orleans Mardi Gras Committee announced it was fearful that California's Hell's Angels Motorcycle Club might be among its unwelcome guests.

January 31. Leading citizens opposed a proposed expressway as a threat to the "historical character" of the Vieux Carré and prepared to sue to prevent its completion.

February 8. Federal government school examiners urged the end of federal financial aid to schools of the St. James Parish for failure to comply with the Civil Rights Act of 1964.

October 9. Excavations for the new Hilton Hotel were reported to cause cracking in various old buildings in the Vieux Carré; excavations were halted by court order and hearings were set.

1967

February 17. It was revealed that New Orleans District Attorney James Garrison was seeking to prove that President Kennedy's assassination was the result of a conspiracy, which had originated in New Orleans and that Lee Harvey Oswald had not been the killer.

June 6. The United States Supreme Court upheld a ruling that the city of New Orleans owed the United States Government $405,903.00 with accumulated interest since it illegally collected that amount as tax on machinery the Chrysler Corporation installed in a government owned ordinance plant. Chrysler had paid the tax under protest at the direction of the Federal authorities.

July 16. Many construction sites in the city were idle due to a serious jurisdictional dispute between unions.

September 6. District Attorney James Garrison accused Chief Justice Earl Warren of trying to suppress the truth about the Kennedy assassination by subverting his investigation.

December 14. The site in the Vieux Carré being excavated for a hotel was sold to other interests.

December 17. New Orleans voters approved a sales tax increase, making the city's total sales tax reach five percent.

1968

January 10. The United States Department of Defense allowed navy personnel to attend segregated festivities in uniform during Mardi Gras week. They were to be considered private individuals.

January 21-23. The New Orleans police arrested E.N. Morial, the first black elected to the Louisiana legislature since the Reconstruction period, and jailed him for alleged public misbehavior. After his release, they apologized.

March 25. Plans were announced to the proposed construction of a 31-story, 500,000 square foot office building in downtown New Orleans.

May 13. A festival of jazz began the celebrations of the 250th anniversary of the founding of the city.

June 5. The city imposed an amusement tax of 20 percent on theaters and movie houses, a 5 percent tax on other forms of amusements.

September 24. The New Orleans police department continued the practice of having policewomen accompany policemen on routine investigations despite protests by policemen's wives and by some policemen.

1969

November 20. The attempt to make New Orleans a free-trade sub-zone for duty-free steel was opposed by national steel companies.

January 18. The dispute over the expressway that would have cut off part of the Vieux Carré and the Jackson Square area from a river view was settled when the Federal Highway Administration approved an alternate plan.

February 6. Nearly 200 people were arrested during the Mardi Gras festivities. The controversies that led to violence included the choice of Danny Kaye rather than a native New Orleanian as the Mardi Gras King and protests by blacks over the floats showing "Zulus" wearing black faces and "parodying" African cultures.

February 6. Floats at the Mardi Gras were incomplete due to the absence of imported items because of a Longshoreman's strike.

March 2. The <u>New Orleans States-Item</u> called for the resignation of District Attorney Garrison, charging that he "perverted justice" in pursuing the case against a New Orleans man, C.L. Shaw, for allegedly conspiring to kill President Kennedy.

June 3. The <u>Times-Picayune</u> publishers announced that the <u>States-Item</u> and the <u>Times-Picayune</u> would be made into separate and autonomous divisions with separate news and editoral staffs.

June 18. The assistant to District Attorney Garrison, C.R. Ward, resigned and began a campaign against Garrison's activities.

June 23. The Port of New Orleans planned the construction of a nine-berth complex, estimated to cost about sixty-four million dollars, to serve container ships.

July 25. The United States Department of Justice filed suit against the New Orleans sub-division of La Kratt Development Corporation for allegedly discriminating against blacks in the sale and financing of homes.

October 21. About 150 New Orleans policemen demonstrated at City Hall for an increase in salaries; officials responded by warning them against striking.

November 10. District Attorney Garrison won reelection to a third term with the support of New Orleans blacks and working class whites.

November 12. New Orleans longshoremen refused to unload highly automated ships.

1970

The population of New Orleans was estimated to be 54.5 percent white and 45.5 percent non-white.

February 10. Trumpet player Al Hirt was hit in the mouth with a brick thrown from the crowd while playing on a float during the Mardi Gras parade.

February 11. Mayor Schiro warned that the Mardi Gras festivities might be discontinued because of widespread violence. He reported that 600 people had been arrested, one person had been killed, and that thousands of "hippies" had created situations difficult to control; rising criticism of the celebration's ideological content and alleged waste of public funds and energy resources were also cited as negative factors endangering its survival.

April 9. Councilman Moon Landrieu was elected mayor on the Democratic ticket, but his Republican opponent, B.C. Toledano, showed surprising strength in the city.

July 2. District Attorney Garrison was arrested in New Orleans. He charged he had been framed, because many in the government did not wish him to continue his investigation of the Kennedy assassination. The list of charges brought against Garrison included bribery and tax evasion.

September 16. The New Orleans police were involved in a shoot-out with a group of blacks in the Desire section of the city near the headquarters of the National Committee to Combat Fascism, the arm of the Black Panther Party. The toll included one youth killed, three wounded, and fourteen arrested; all were blacks.

October 7. The United States Senate Subcommittee on Internal Security held a hearing on urban guerilla warfare; among others, officers from the New Orleans police testified on the activities of the Black Panthers in their city.

December 6. A group of sixteen New Orleans clergymen

and other citizens protested the methods used in the incident at the Desire Housing Project, claiming that the police gained entry into the alleged Black Panther apartment by wearing clerical garb. Mayor Landrieu pledged there would not be a repetition of the use of such tactics by the police.

December 7. Preparations began for the celebration of Rex's Centennial at the Mardi Gras festivities only a few months away.

DOCUMENTS

The following annotated documentary section is made up of carefully selected source materials, such as scholars use to write history. By studying these sample texts, the student will become involved in the processes of historical interpretation which depend upon a critical reading of a great variety of such documents.

Limits of space have greatly reduced the length of many of the documents included in this section. However, the reader will profit by engaging in the scholar's basic task of discovering the complete texts by referring on his own to the sources cited in each case and, in some cases, to the bibliography section of this work.

NEW ORLEANS: FROM EMPIRE TO MUNICIPALITY: 1539-1718

The foundation and growth of the city as an independent municipality took place before the Americans arrived to claim the capital of their "purchase" in 1803. That complicated history of the clash of European empires in the New World and the evolution of this imperial capital is admirably summarized in the almost forgotten doctoral dissertation of William W. Howe, written at Johns Hopkins University in the late 1880's.

Source: William W. Howe, Municipal History of New Orleans in Johns Hopkins University Studies in Historical and Political Science, Baltimore, 1889.

For nearly two centuries after the discovery of America, the Mississippi River remained almost unknown; and it was not until the year 1682 that LaSalle picked his perilous path from Canada by the way of Lake Michigan and the Illinois, and descended the great stream to its mouth. He was exploring under the patronage of Louis Fourteenth, and gave the name of Louisiana to the vast valley.

The first permanent settlement made by the French in this new domain was established at Biloxi, now in the State of Mississippi, which was founded by Iberville in 1699, and was the chief town of the colony until 1702, when Bienville moved headquarters to the Mobile River. The soil in the neighborhood of Biloxi is sandy and sterile and the settlers depended mainly on supplies from France and St. Domingo. The French Government, distant and necessarily ignorant of the details of pioneer life, sent instructions to search for gold and pearls. The wool of buffaloes was also pointed out to the colonial officials as the future staple commodity of the country, and they were directed to have a number of these animals penned and tamed. It is hardly necessary to say that but little profit was ever realized from the search for gold and pearls, or from the shearing of buffaloes.

In 1712 the entire commerce of Louisiana, with a considerable control in its government, was granted by charter to Anthony Crozat, an eminent French merchant. The territory is described in this charter as that possessed by the Crown between Old and New Mexico, and Carolina, and all the settlements, ports, roads and rivers therein, principally the port and road of Dauphine Island, formerly called Massacre Island, the river St. Louis, previously called the Mississippi, from the Sea to the Illinois, the river St. Philip, previously called the Missouri, the river St. Jerome, previously called the Wabash, with all the lands, lakes and rivers mediately or immediately draining into any part of the river St. Louis or Mississippi. The territory thus described was to be and remain included under the style of the government of Louisiana, and to be a dependency of the government of New France to which it was subordinated. By another provision of this charter, the laws, edicts and ordinances of the realm and the Custom of Paris were extended to Louisiana.

The grant to Crozat, which seemed so magnificent on paper, extending as it did from the Alleghenies to the Rocky Mountains, and from the Rio Grande and the Gulf to the far Northwest, proved of little use or value to him, and of little benefit to the colony; and in 1718 he surrendered the privilege. In the same year the charter of the Western or Mississippi Company was registered in the Parliament of Paris. The history of this scheme, with which John Law was connected, is well known. The exclusive commerce of Louisiana was granted to the Company for twenty-five years, and a monopoly of the beaver trade of Canada, together with other extraordinary privileges; and it entered at once on its new domain. Bienville was again appointed Governor. He had become satisfied that the chief city of the colony ought to be established on the Mississippi, and so in 1718 the site of New Orleans was selected. Its location was plainly determined by the fact that it lies between the River and Lake Ponchartrain, with the Bayou St. John and the Bayou Sauvage or Gentilly affording navigation for a large part of the distance from the lake towards the river. And even at this early day there was a plan of constructing jetties at the mouth of the Mississippi and so making New Orleans the deep water port of the Gulf. Pauger, the engineer, reported a plan for removing the bar at the entrance of one of the passes, by the same system in principle as the one recently and successfully adopted by Mr. James B. Eads under the Act of Congress of 1875.

Le Page du Pratz visited the place during the same year, and took up a plantation on the Bayou St. John, "a short half league from the site of the Capital," which he says was "then marked only by a shed covered with leaves of latanier," the building, such as it was, being occupied by the Commandant of the Post.

The seat of government was finally removed to New Orleans in August, 1722, and when Charlevoix visited the place, in December, 1723, it contained about one hundred houses, mostly cabins. The well-known map of 1728 shows the town protected by a levee and laid off in rectangular form, having eleven squares front on the river by a depth of six squares.

In 1732 the Western Company surrendered its grant. In 1763 a secret treaty was signed at Paris by which France ceded to Spain all that portion of Louisiana which lay west of the Mississippi together with the City of New Orleans, "and the Island on which it stands." The war between England, France and Spain was terminated by the treaty of Paris in February, 1764. By the terms of this treaty the boundary between the French and British possessions in North America was fixed by a line drawn along the middle of the River Mississippi from its source to the River Iberville and thence by a line in the middle of that stream of lake Maurepas and Ponchartrain to the Sea. France ceded to Great Britain the River and Port of Mobile and everything she had possessed on the left bank of the Mississippi except the town of New Orleans and the Island on which it stood. As all that part of Louisiana not thus ceded to Great Britain had been already transferred to Spain, it followed that France had now parted with the last inch of soil she had owned on the continent of North America.

From its foundation up to this date New Orleans was governed by the Superior Council, a body which had general control of the colony but at the same time took special charge of the administration and police of the Capital. This council had been first established under Crozat, in 1712, by royal edict with powers equivalent to those of similar bodies in St. Domingo and Martinique, and consisted of the governor and commissary ordonnateur; its existence being limited to three years from the day of its first meeting. In September, 1716, it was reorganized by a perpetual edict and composed of the governor general and intendant of New France, the governor of Louisiana, a senior counsellor, the King's lieutenant, two puisné counsellors, an attorney general and a clerk. The edict gave to the council all the powers exercised by similar bodies in the other colonies. Its sessions were directed to be held monthly. One of its most important functions was judicial, for it determined all cases, civil and criminal, in the last resort. In civil cases three members constituted a quorum, in criminal cases five. There was a possibility of popular representation in the provision that, in the absence and lawful excuse of members, a quorum might be completed by calling in notables.

The transfer of the colony to the Western Company called for another change in the organization of the Council; and by an edict of September 1719 it was made to consist of such directors of that Company as might be in the provinces, together with the commandant general, a senior counsellor, the two King's lieutenants, three other counsellors, an attorney general and a clerk.

On the surrender of the charter of the Western Company in 1732, the Council was again remodeled by royal letters patent of May 7th. The members were declared to be the governor general of New France, the governor and commissary of Louisiana, the King's lieutenant, the town mayor of New Orleans, six counsellors, an attorney general and a clerk. In August, 1742, the increase of trade had caused such an increase of litigation that it was deemed necessary to add to the judicial force; and accordingly by royal letters patent the commissary ordonnateur was directed to appoint four assessors to serve for a period of four years, —their duties being to report in cases referred to them, or to sit when they were required to complete a quorum or to break the dead-lock of a tie vote.

Under such a regime New Orleans was hardly a municipal corporation in any English or American sense. It certainly had at that time no municipal charter. It resembled in some respects a commune, and has been alluded to by the Supreme Court of Louisiana as having been at that time a city.

THE "BLACK CODE" OF LOUISIANA, 1724

In the "Black Code" (Code Noir), the first governor of the French colony of New Orleans, Bienville, provided the plantation slave economy with its fundamental laws relating to the status of the slave. But, as the selection below indicates, the code also dealt with the religious constitution of the colony. After 1803, it was perpetuated in the code of American Louisiana.

Source: Alcée Fortier, A History of Louisiana, New York: 1904.

In March, 1724, the King issued at Versailles an "Edict concerning the negro slaves in Louisiana." This is generally known as the "Black Code," which remained in force in colonial times, and of which some of the provisions were incorporated into the code of American Louisiana. The edict, according to the official certificate of Rossard, clerk of the Superior Council, was read, recorded, and published in New Orleans on September 10, 1724. The preamble to this edict is given here in full, to show the forms of such documents.

Louis, by the Grace of God, King of France and of Navarre, to all present and to come, greeting. The Directors of the Company of the Indies having represented to us that the Province and colony of Louisiana is considerably established, by a large number of our subjects, who use slaves for the cultivation of the lands, We have judged that it behooves our authority and our justice, for the preservation of this colony, to establish there a law, and certain rules, to maintain there the discipline of the Catholic Apostolic and Roman Church, and to order about what concerns the state and condition of the slaves in the said Islands, and desiring to provide for this, and to make known to our subjects who inhabit there and who shall settle there in the future, that although they inhabit climes infinitely remote, We are always present, by the extent of our power and by our application to succor them. Actuated by these causes and others, by the advice of our Council, and by our certain knowledge, full power and Royal authority, We have said, decreed, and ordered, We say, decree, and order, wish and it pleases us, the following.

ARTICLE I orders that the edict of 1615 be applied to Louisiana, and that all Jews who may have established their religion there be expelled within three months, under penalty of confiscation of body and property.

ARTICLE II orders that all slaves in the province be instructed and baptized in the Catholic religion.

ARTICLE III forbids the exercise of any other religion than the Catholic.

ARTICLE IV forbids the employment of any overseer who shall not be a Catholic, under penalty of confiscation of the negroes and punishment of the overseer.

ARTICLE V orders Sundays and holidays to be regularly observed, and forbids all work by master or slaves, under penalty of confiscation of slaves and punishment of masters. The slaves, however, may be sent marketing.

ARTICLE VI forbids marriage of whites with slaves, and concubinage of whites and manumitted or free-born blacks with slaves, and imposes penalties.

ARTICLE VII orders to be observed, for marriages of free persons as well as of slaves, the solemnities of the ordinance of Blois and of the edict of 1639. The consent of the parents of the slave is not necessary, but only that of the master.

ARTICLE VIII forbids curates to celebrate marriages of slaves without consent of the masters, and forbids masters to force their slaves to marry against their will.

ARTICLE IX enacts that children born from the marriages of slaves shall belong to the master of the mother.

ARTICLE X enacts that if the husband be a slave and the wife a free woman, the children shall be free like their mother. If the husband be free and the wife a slave, the children shall be slaves.

ARTICLE XI orders that master shall have baptized slaves buried in consecrated ground; those who die without being baptized to be buried at night in a neighboring field.

ARTICLE XII forbids slaves to carry offensive weapons or heavy sticks, under penalty of the whip and confiscation of the weapons in favor of the person seizing them. Slaves that are sent hunting by their masters, and carry notes or known marks, are excepted.

ARTICLE XIII forbids slaves belonging to different masters to assemble in crowds, by day or by night, under pretext of weddings or other causes, either at one of their masters or elsewhere, and still less on the highways or secluded places, under penalty of corporal punishment, which shall not be less than the whip and the fleur-de-lys; and in case of repetition of the offense and other aggravating circumstances, capital punishment may be applied, at the discretion of the judges. It also commands all subjects of the King, whether officers or not, to seize and arrest the offenders and conduct them to prison, although there be no judgment against them. . . .

ARTICLE XVII orders seizure of goods that are offered for sale by slaves without permission or mark.

ARTICLE XVIII orders officers of the Superior Council to give their advice about the provisions and the food to be furnished the slaves. It also forbids masters to give any kind of brandy in lieu of food and clothing.

ARTICLE XIX forbids masters to abstain from feeding and clothing their slaves, by permitting them to work for their own account on a certain day of the week.

ARTICLE XX authorizes slaves to give information against their masters, if not properly fed or clad, or if treated inhumanly.

ARTICLE XXI orders slaves disabled from working by old age, sickness, or otherwise, to be provided for by their masters, otherwise they shall be sent to the nearest hospital, to which the masters shall pay eight cents a day for each slave, and the hospital shall have a lien on the plantations of the masters.

ARTICLE XXII declares that slaves can have nothing that does not belong to their masters, in whatever way acquired.

ARTICLE XXIII orders that masters be held responsible for what their slaves have done by their command.

ARTICLE XXIV forbids slaves from exercising public functions, from serving as arbitrators or experts, from giving testimony except in default of white people, and from ever serving as witnesses for or against their masters.

ARTICLE XXV forbids slaves from being parties to civil suits or complainants in criminal cases. Their masters shall act for them in civil cases and demand reparation or punishment for outrages and excesses committed against them.

ARTICLE XXVI orders prosecution of slaves in criminal cases in the same manner as for free persons, with exceptions hereafter mentioned.

ARTICLE XXVII. Any slave who shall have struck his master, his mistress, or the husband of his mistress, or their children, so as to produce a bruise or shedding of blood in the face, shall be put to death.

ARTICLE XXVIII. Outrages or acts of violence against free persons committed by slaves shall be punished with severity, and even with death if the case require it.

THE TREATY OF PARIS, 1803: LOUISIANA PURCHASE

Although undoubtedly Napoleon I welcomed the 15 million dollars he received for the cession of the Louisiana Territory to the United States, the treaty itself emphasized the benefits to be derived from mutual cooperation and trade and omits altogether any mention of the financial transaction.

Source: The Louisiana Historical Quarterly, Vol. 2, No. 2, New Orleans: 1919.

TREATY BETWEEN THE FRENCH REPUBLIC AND THE UNITED STATES, CONCERNING THE CESSION OF LOUISIANA, SIGNED AT PARIS THE 30th OF APRIL, 1803.

The President of the United States of America, and the first Consul of the French Republic, in the name of the French people, desiring to remove all source of misunderstanding relative to objects of discussion, mentioned in the second and fifth articles of the convention of the 8th vendemiaire, an 9 (30th of September, 1800), relative to the rights claimed by the United States, in virtue of the treaty concluded at Madrid the 27th of October, 1795, between his Catholic Majesty and the said United States, and willing to strengthen the union and friendship which at the time of the said convention was happily reestablished between the two nations, have respectively named their plenipotentiaries; to-wit, the President of the United States of America, by and with the advice and consent of the Senate of the said States, Robert R. Livingston, Minister Plenipotentiary of the United States, and James Monroe, Minister Plenipotentiary and Envoy Extraordinary of the said States, near the government of the French Republic; and the First Consul, in the name of the French people, the French citizen Barbe Marbois, Minister of the Public Treasury, who after having respectively exchanged their full powers, have agreed to the following articles:

"Article 1st.   Whereas, by the article the third of the treaty concluded at the St. Ildephonso, the 9th Vendemiaire, an 9 (1st October, 1800), between the First Consul of the French Republic and his Catholic Majesty, it was agreed as follows: 'His Catholic Majesty promises and engages, on his part, to retrocede to the French Republic, six months after the full and entire execution of the conditions and stipulations herein relative to his Royal Highness the Duke of Parma, the colony or province of Louisiana, with the same extent that it now has in the hands of Spain, and that it had when France possessed it; and such as it should be after the treaties subsequently entered into between Spain and other States.'   And, whereas, in pursuance of the treaty, and particularly of the third article, the French Republic has an incontestable title to the domain and to the possession of the said territory:

The First Consul of the French Republic, desiring to give to the United States a strong proof of his friendship, doth hereby cede to the said United States, in the name of the French Republic, for ever and in full sovereignty, the said territory, with all its rights and appurtenances, as fully and in the same manner as they had been acquired by the French Republic in virtue of the above-mentioned treaty concluded with his Catholic Majesty.

"Art. 2nd. In the cession made by the preceding article are included the adjacent islands belonging to Louisiana, all public lots and squares, vacant lands, and all public buildings, fortifications, barracks, and other edifices which are not private property. The archives, papers, and documents, relative to the domain and sovereignty of Louisiana and its dependencies, will be left in the possession of the commissaries of the United States, and copies will be afterwards given in due form to the magistrates and municipal officers of such of the said papers and documents as may be necessary to them.

"Art. 3rd. The inhabitants of the ceded territory shall be incorporated in the Union of the United States, and admitted as soon as possible, according to the principles of the Federal Constitution, to the enjoyment of all the rights, advantages and immunities of citizens of the United States; and in the mean time they shall be maintained and protected in the free enjoyment of their liberty, property, and the religion which they profess.

"Art. 4th. There shall be sent by the government of France a Commissary to Louisiana, to the end that he do every act necessary, as well to receive from the officers of his Catholic Majesty the said country and its dependencies, in the name of the French Republic, if it had not been already done, as to transmit it in the name of the French to the commissary or agent of the United States.

"Art. 5th. Immediately after the ratification of the present treaty by the President of the United States, and in case that of the First Consul shall have been previously obtained, the Commissary of the French Republic shall remit all the military posts of New Orleans and other parts of the ceded territory to the Commissary or Commissaries named by the President to take possession; the troops whether of France or Spain, who may be there shall cease to occupy any military post from the time of taking possession, and shall be embarked as soon as possible, in the course of three months after the ratification of this treaty.

"Art. 6th. The United States promise to execute such treaties and articles as may have been agreed between Spain and the tribes and nations of Indians, until, by mutual consent of the United States and the said tribes of nations, other suitable articles shall have been agreed upon.

"Art. 7th. As it is reciprocally advantageous to the commerce of France and the United States to encourage the communication of both nations for a limited time in the country ceded by the present treaty, until general arrangements relative to the commerce of both nations may be agreed between the contracting parties, that the French ships coming directly from France or any of her colonies, loaded only with the produce or manufacture of France or her said colonies; and the ships of Spain coming directly from Spain or any of her colonies, loaded only with the produce or manufactures of Spain or her colonies, shall be admitted during the space of twelve years in the port of New Orleans and in all other legal ports of entry within the ceded territory, in the same manner as the ships of the United States coming directly from France or Spain or any of their colonies, without being subject to any other or greater duty on merchandise, or other or greater tonnage than those paid by the citizens of the United States.

"During the space of time above-mentioned, no other nation shall have a right to the same privileges in the ports of the ceded territory; the twelve years shall commence three months after the exchange of ratifications, if it shall take place in France, or three months after it shall have been notified at Paris to the French government, if it shall take place in the United States: it is, however, well understood that the object of the above article is to favor the manufactures, commerce, freight, and navigation of France and of Spain, so far as relates to the importations that the French and Spanish shall make into the said ports of the United States, without in any sort affecting the regulations that the United States may make concerning the exportation of the produce and merchandise of the United States, or any right they may have to make such regulations.

"Art. 8th. In future, and for ever after the expiration of the twelve years, the ships of France shall be treated upon the footing of the most favored nations in the ports above-mentioned.

"Art. 9th. The particular convention, signed this day by the respective Ministers, having for its object to provide for the payment of debts due to the citizens of the United States by the French Republic, prior to the 30th of September, 1800 (8th Vendemiaire, an 9), is approved, and to have its execution in the same manner as if it had been inserted in the present treaty; and it shall be ratified in the same form, and in the same time, so that the one shall not be ratified distinct from the other.

"Another particular convention, signed at the same date as the present treaty, relative to the definitive rule between the contracting parties, is in the like manner approved, and will be ratified in the same form, and in the same time, and jointly.

"Art. 10th. The present treaty shall be ratified in good and due form, and the ratifications shall be exchanged in the space of six months after the date of the signature by the Ministers Plenipotentiary, or sooner if possible.

"In faith whereof, the respective Plenipotentiaries have signed these articles in the French and English languages; declaring, nevertheless, that the present treaty was originally agreed to in the French language; and have thereunto put their seals.

"Done at Paris, the tenth day of Floreal, in the eleventh year of the French Republic, and the 30th of April, 1803.

"ROBERT R. LIVINGSTON,
"JAMES MONROE,
"BARBE MARBOIS."

THE AMERICANIZATION of NEW ORLEANS, 1803-1804

The following four letters from the Letter Books of William C.C. Claiborne (1775-1817), American governor of the Territory of Orleans, to James Madison reveal some American attitudes towards the society of the new territory.

Source: Dunbar Rowland, <u>Official Letter Books of W.C.C. Claiborne: 1801-1816</u>, Jackson, Miss.: 1917.

New Orleans, December 20th, 1803

SIR,

    The Letters from the American Commissioners will inform you that we are now in possession of this City. The Standard of my Country was this day unfurled here amidst the reiterated acclamations of thousands. And if I may judge by professions and appearance, the Government of the United States is received with joy and gratitude by the People. I shall write to you more fully by the next Mail. At present let it suffice to say, that the surrender of the province to us has been happily accomplished under as favourable omens as we could wish.

    Accept assurances of my sincere esteem and high consideration.

Wm. C. C. Claiborne

The Honble.
James Madison
Secty. of State

New Orleans, January 10th, 1804

Sir,

    The more I become acquainted with the inhabitants of this Province, the more I am convinced of their unfitness for a representative Government. The Credulity of the People is indeed great, and a virtuous Magistrate resting entirely for Support on the Suffrages and good will of his fellow Citizens in this quarter would often be exposed to immediate ruin by the Machinations of a few base individuals who with some exertion and address might make many of the people think against their will, and act against their Interests.

    God forbid that I should recommend for this people Political provisions under which oppression of any kind could be practised with impunity, by persons in power, but I do think that their own happiness renders it advisable that they remain for some years under the immediate Guardianship of

Congress, and that for the present a local and temporary Government for Louisiana upon principles somewhat Similar to our Territorial Government in their first grade be established.

I have discovered with regret that a strong partiality for the French Government still exists among many of the inhabitants of this City. I have learned that in some circles a Sentiment is cherished, that at the close of the War between England and France, the great Buonaparte will again raise his standard in this country. For my part, I attach no importance to this little Political Speculation. It is directed more by the wishes of those who busy themselves on the subject, than by any reasonable ground of expectation.

The harmony of Society here has experienced some interruptions since my last letter. A <u>Fracas</u> took place at a Public Ball, on Thursday last, which altho' it arose from trifling causes, has occasioned some warmth. It originated in a contest between some young Americans and Frenchmen, whether the American or French Dances should have a preference. I believe this affair is at an end, but being desirous at the present juncture of communicating every circumstance which might have a political tendency, I have deemed it worthy of mentioning. I have as yet incurred but little expense in the exercise of my temporary authority. A prudent economy shall be kept constantly in view. I found it necessary to employ an Interpreter to the French and Spanish Languages, and a private Secretary, which together with the expense of printing constitute at present the principal items in my account. Accept assurances of great respect and sincere esteem.

Wm. C.C. Claiborne

The Honble.
James Madison
Secty. of State

New Orleans, January 24th, 1804

Sir,

The period allowed by the Treaty for the withdrawing of the French and Spanish forces from the ceded Territory expires this day, and still little or no preparation is made for an Embarkation. The Spaniards have in this City (I understand) about two hundred Men, and near thirty officers; they retain a part of the Barracks, and the Public Ware Houses are still occupied by their Military Stores. But otherwise the United States experience no injury by their remaining. The Spanish Officers since the delivery of the City to the American Commissioners have conducted themselves with great propriety, and manifested a friendly disposition to the Authorities of the United States. The Spanish Troops are in excellent subordination, and have not in the least degree interrupted the harmony of the City. I cannot speak equally favourable of the French forces; these are indeed inconsiderable, I believe they have no soldiers, but few Sailors, and only <u>eight</u> or <u>ten</u> <u>officers</u>; but some of these are mischievous, riotous, disorderly characters, and have contributed greatly to interrupt the harmony of this City. There are also in New Orleans between twenty and thirty young adventurers from Bordeaux and St. Domingo who are troublesome to this Society, they are men of some information, desperate fortunes, and inflated with the Idea of the invincibility of Buonaparte, and the power of the French nation; they feel mortified at the possession of this Province by the United States, and seem determined to sour the Inhabitants as much as possible with the American Government. The Means they use are the dissemination of falsehood (which among the uniformed and credulous pass current) and incessant efforts to foment divisions among the Creoles of the Country and the natives of the United States who are here. These disorderly Men have an extensive range for the display of their Mischievous dispositions, the language, manners and habits of the people here are French, and a strong partiality still exists for the French Nation; added to this, the ignorance and credulity of the mass of the people, and here, Sir, is the great Source of Misfortune. Until information is more generally diffused, the American Government will not have fair play in this Province, and a virtuous magistrate may be ruined by misrepresentation, for the people may be made to believe any thing.

I consider that the diffusion of information among this people is so essential to their political happiness and to the Welfare of the American Government, that I would think it wise policy in Congress to appropriate one hundred thousand dollars annually for the encouragement of Education in Louisiana.

The other day I granted permission to the Mayor of the City to remove the dirt from some useless outworks adjoining the Fort to repair a breach in the Levee. A citizen of this place, who claims [ownership of] the land on which the fort is erected, remonstrated, and says his private rights are violated, and that he must look to the President for redress. Thus you see Sir, that it will not be an easy task to give satisfaction to these uninformed people.

Accept assurances of my high and respectful consideration.

                                            Wm. C.C. Claiborne

The Honble.
James Madison
Secty. of State

                                       New Orleans, January 31st, 1804

Sir,

A Vessel arrived at this Post a few days ago with fifty African Negroes for Sale. Being unwilling to permit so barbarous a Traffic, if my powers Authorized me to prevent it, I immediately applied to the late Spanish Contador at his place, a man of great integrity of character, for information as to the Laws and customs of Spain relating to the African trade. Learning from him that the bringing of African Slaves to Louisiana had been permitted by the Spanish Authorities and doubting whether I was vested with power to forbid their Sale, the importer has been left to pursue his own wishes.

The Public Ball room has been the Theatre of great Disorder. During the Winter Season, there has for many years been a Ball twice a week. Every white Male visits it who will pay at the door 50 cents, and the Ladies of every Rank attend these assemblies in great numbers. The Consequence is that the company is generally composed of a very heterogeneous mass. To keep order at these Balls (under the Spanish Government) a Strong guard was Stationed at the Ball room, and on the first appearance of disorder the persons concerned were committed.

On my arrival at New Orleans, I found the people very Solicitous to maintain their Public Ball establishment, and to convince them that the American Government felt no disposition to break in upon their amusements (as had been reported by some mischievous persons) General Wilkinson and myself occasionally attended these assemblies.

Under the Spanish Government, the Governor General was the Regulator of the Balls, but this Gallant duty I have cheerfully surrendered to the Municipality of the City. I fear you will suppose that I am wanting in respect in calling your attention to the Balls of New Orleans, but I do assure you Sir, that they occupy much of the Public mind, and from them have proceeded the greatest embarrassments which have heretofore attended my administration.

Accept assurances of my great respect and high consideration.

            Wm. C.C. Claiborne

The Honble.
James Madison
Secty. of State

BENJAMIN HENRY LATROBE'S IMPRESSIONS OF NEW ORLEANS
1818

Benjamin Henry Labrobe (1764-1820) arrived in New Orleans in 1818 after his son had died the year before of yellow fever while building the city's waterworks. These impressions, from the eye of the master architect whose Greek Revival buildings adorned America's early cities, are as precise as the Greek forms he so much admired. Two years after his arrival in the city, he followed his son in death from yellow fever.

Source: Benjamin Henry Latrobe, Journal of Benjamin Henry Latrobe, New York, 1905.

What is the state of society in New Orleans? is one of many questions which I am required to answer by a friend, who seems not to be aware that this question is equivalent to that of Shakespeare's Polonius. He might as well ask: What is the shape of a cloud? The state of society at any time here is puzzling. There are, in fact, three societies here -- first the French, second the American, and third the mixed. The French side is not exactly what it was at the change of government, and the American is not strictly what it is in the Atlantic cities. The opportunity of growing rich by more active, extensive, and intelligent modes of agriculture and commerce has diminished the hospitality, destroyed the leisure, and added more selfishness to the character of the creoles. The Americans, coming hither to make money and considering their residence as temporary, are doubly active in availing themselves of the enlarged opportunities of becoming wealthy which the place offers. On the whole, the state of society is similar to that of every city rapidly rising into wealth, and doing so much, and such fast increasing business, that no man can be said to have a moment's leisure. Their business is to make money. They are in an eternal bustle. Their limbs, their heads, and their hearts move to that sole object. Cotton and tobacco, buying and selling, and all the rest of the occupation of a money-making community, fill their time and give the habit of their minds. The post which comes in and goes out three times a week renders those days, more than the others, days of oppressive exertion. I have been received with great hospitality, have dined out almost every day, but the time of a late dinner and a short sitting after it have been the only periods during which I could make any acquaintance with the gentlemen of the place. As it is now the Carnival, every evening is closed with a ball, or a play, or a concert. I have been to two of each.

To entitle a stranger to describe the character of a society more is required than to have looked at it superficially, and through the medium of habits acquired elsewhere. More than a superficial use of the senses is required to ascertain facts of which the senses are the only judges. The great fault of travelers, I was going to say, especially of English travelers -- because we Americans have suffered most by the false accounts of our contry -- is to impose first impressions upon themselves and the public for the actual states of things. To determine upon the relative moral or political character of a community requires more time, more talent, and more philosophical investigation of the history of its habits, and of those causes of them over which no control can be exercised, than traveling bookmakers possess or can command.

It would therefore be very impertinent in me, after ten days' residence only, to call anything which I may put into these brochures by a name more decided than my impressions respecting New Orleans.

My impressions, then, as to the surface of female society, are that there are collected in New Orleans at a ball, many women, below the age of twenty-four or twenty-five, of more correct and beautiful features, and with faces and figures more fit for the sculptor, than I ever recollect to have seen together elsewhere in the same number. A few of them are perfect, and a great majority are far above the mere agreeable. I have said faces for the sculptor, not altogether for the painter, for the lilies have banished the roses. The Anglican slang of a painted French woman does not apply here. A few American ladies, not long resident here, had rosy cheeks, but very few. The French creoles are universally of healthy color, fair, but the cheeks are of the color of the forehead. At a <u>bal paré</u> the number of brunettes was small, and my attention being alive to the subject, I could not see one face that had the slightest tinge of rouge. There was a face and a head, the beautiful hair of which was decorated with a single white rose, surmounting a figure exquisitely formed and moving with perfect grace, belonging to some young lady apparently of eighteen, whom I am glad I do not know, but which was as perfect in all respects as anything I have ever seen in or out of marble.

The dancing of the ladies was what is to be expected of French women; that of the gentleman, what Lord Chesterfield would have called, too good for gentlemen. I hope and believe that we Americans have qualities which make up for our deficiency in dancing, a deficiency which marked those young Americans that were upon the floor.

I have never been in a public assembly altogether better conducted. No confusion, no embarrassment as to the sets having, in their turn, a right to occupy the floor, no bustle of managers, no obtrusive solicitors of public attention.

Altogether the impression was highly favorable. The only nuisances was a tall, ill-dressed black in the music gallery, who played the tambourine standing up, and in a forced and vile voice called the figures as they changed.

The French population in Louisiana is said to be only 20,000, in the city not above 5,000 or 6,000. The increase is of Americans. Some French have come hither since the return of the Bourbons, but they did not find themselves at home; some joined General Lallemand in his settlement on Trinity River, a few remained so as sensibly to increase the French population. The accession, if worth mentioning, did not exceed the emigration which has taken place of those who did not like the American Government, or had amassed fortunes and have returned to France or settled in the West Indian islands. Since the breaking of Lallemand's colony, a few have returned to New Orleans, but so few that they are not a perceptible quantity, even in the comparatively small French community.

On the other hand, Americans are pouring in daily, not in families, but in large bodies. In a few years, therefore, this will be an American town. What is good and bad in the French manners and opinions must give way, and the American notions of right and wrong, of convenience and inconvenience, will take their place.

When this period arrives, it will be folly to say that they are better or worse than they now are. They will be changed, but they will be changed into that which is more agreeable to the new population than what now exists. But a man who fancies that he has seen the world on more sides than one cannot help wishing that a mean, an average character, of society may grow out of the intermixture of the French and American manners.

Such a consummation is, perhaps, to be more devoutly wished than hoped for. There is a lady, and I am told a leading one among the Americans, who can speak French well, but is determined never to condescend to speak to the French ladies in their language, although in New York she prided herself on her knowing that language. Many of the leading gentlemen, when not talking of tobacco or cotton, find it very amusing to abuse and ridicule French morals, French manners, and French houses. In truth, there is evidently growing up a party spirit, which in time will give success to the view of the Americans, and everything French will in time disappear. Even the miserable patois of the creoles will be heard only in the cypress swamps. . . .

A VIEW OF NEW ORLEANS
1835

The following selection, written by the novelist Joseph H. Ingraham, describes some of the aspects of New Orleans' gracious and opulent way of life.

Source: Joseph H. Ingraham, The South-West By A Yankee, New York, 1835, vol. I. pp 88-116.

As we sallied from our hotel to commence our first tour of sight seeing, the vast city was just waking into life. Our sleepy servants were opening the shutters, and up and down the street a hundred of their drowsy brethren were at the same enlightening occupation. Black women, with huge baskets of rusks, rolls and other appurtenances of the breakfast table, were crying, in loud shrill French, their "stock in trade," followed by milk-criers of everything but tears: for they all seemed as merry as the morning, saluting each other gayly as they met, "Bo'shoo Mumdasl" -- "Moshoo! adieu," &c. &c., and shooting their rude shafts of African wit at each other with much vivacity and humor.

We turned down Canal-street -- the broadest in New Orleans, and destined to be the most magnificent. Its breadth I do not know, correctly, but it is certainly one half wider than Broadway opposite the Park. -- Through its centre runs a double row of young trees, which, when they arrive at maturity, will form the finest mall in the United States, unless the esplanade -- a beautifull mall as the south part of the city, should excel it.

From the head of Canal-street we entered Levee-street, leaving the custom house, a large, plain yellow stuccoed building upon our right, near which is a huge, dark coloured, unshapely pile of brick, originally erected for a Bethel church for seamen, but never finished, and seldom occupied, except by itinerant showmen, with their wonders. Levee-street had already begun to assume a bustling, commerce-like appearance. The horse-drays were trundling rapidly by, sometimes four abreast, racing to different parts of the Levee for their loads -- and upon each was mounted a ragged negro, who, as Jehu-like he drove along, standing upright and unsupported, resembled "Phaeton in the suds" -- rather than "Phaeton the god-like." . . . A French coffee-house is a place well worth visiting by a stranger. . . . As the coffee houses here do not differ materially from each other except in size and richness of decoration, though some of them certainly are more fashionable resorts than others, the description of one of them will enable you perhaps to form some idea of other similar establishments in this city. Though their usual denomination is "coffee-house," they have no earthly, whatever may be their spiritual, right to such a distinction; it is merely a "nomme de profession," assumed, I know not for what object. We entered from the street, after passing round a large Venetian screen within the door, into a spacious room, lighted by numerous lamps, at the extremity of which stood an extensive bar, arranged in addition to the usual array of glass ware, most of them of the most licentious description, and though many of their subjects were classical, of a voluptuous and luxurious character. This is French taste however. There are suspended in the Exchange in Chartres-street -- one of the most magnificent and public rooms in the city -- paintings which, did they occupy an equally conspicuous situation in Merchant's Hall, in Boston, would be instantly defaced by the populace.

Around the room, beneath the paintings, were arranged many small tables, at most of which three of four individuals were seated, some alternately sipping negus and puffing their segars, which are as indispensable necessaries to a Creole at all times, as his right hand, eye-brows, and left shoulders in conversation. Others were reading newspapers, and occasionally assisting their comprehension of abstruse paragraphs, by hot "coffee," alias warm punch and slings, with which, on little japanned salvers, the active attendants were flying in all directions through the spacious room, at the beck and call of customers. The large circular bar was surrounded by a score of noisy applicants for the liquid treasures which held out to them such strong temptations. . . .

TWO SEASONS AT THE ST. CHARLES THEATRE
1841 and 1845

Sol Smith, an important theatrical manager in the South during the first half of the nineteenth century, lived in New Orleans and was involved in its theatrical life. In these selections, Smith discusses two seasons centered upon the most opulent of the city's theaters, the St. Charles.

Source: Sol Smith, <u>Theatrical Management For Thirty Years With Anecdotal Sketches</u>, New York, 1868.

In return for your theatrical information from the East, I must tell you something of the doings in this region.

The St. Charles has not been doing well this season, except during the engagement of Power, and two nights of a brilliant star which burst out upon the boards of the "temple" of the legitimate, bearing the sparkling name of Dimond, a nigger dancer, whose benefit was good; and after that, under the auspices of Barnum, they got up a humbug dancing-match for a pretended wager of $500 a side, and introduced a supernumerary, with his face blacked, to dance with and be beaten by that jewel of dancers, which produced a return (I should think) of nearly $2000!

The weather has been awful for the past six weeks, and has injured the business at both of the theatres very much. "Our house" has held up its head in all weathers, and breasted the storms manfully, not having experienced one failing week; yet our expenses are enormous. Since I last wrote you, we have added Fogg and Stickney's equestrian company to ours, at an expense of nearly $1000 per week. We did this more to prevent their going to the other house than from any gain we expected to derive from the arrangement. I took a circus company, made up of selections from the two troupes, to Natchez, where they performed seven nights to a receipt of $1850, which relieved the concern here of the expense of twenty-three people and twelve horses for nearly two weeks. The two equestrian companies are now performing in the Third Municipality, down by the United States Mint, but are not "coining money," as the saying is; yet the receipts there lighten the expenses here, while Mrs. Fanny Fitzwilliam, the "bright particular" luminary, is cramming the American every night, and throwing from 900 to 1000 people into fits (of laughter), and causing them to forget the hard times, short crops, and every thing else of a disagreeable nature. Isn't she a darling of an actress?

Mr. Caldwell is playing an engagement at his own theatre, but with poor success, which I am sorry for, for he is a fine comedian, and we shall not soon "look upon his like again." Mr. Ranger failed signally at the St. Charles; Buckstone ditto.

Fanny Ellsler has not arranged with any of the N.O. managers yet, but all accounts agree she is coming here soon from Havana. She now asks only $1000 per night! and it is at present uncertain which establishment is to be ruined by her. I hope not ours.

If I had not known you, I should have stared at your getting up "Norma" in so short a time; but, having witnessed your efforts on former occasions, when we have been in a hurry to produce musical pieces, I shall not wonder at any thing you may hereafter do in the musical line. . . .

The New Orleans season of 1846-7 witnessed a continuation of the prosperity which had now become an assured fact. Business not only came up to a paying point, but went considerably beyond it. Stars this season, Wallack, Mrs. Mowatt (with E.L. Davenport, a fine actor), Murdoch, Anderson, Collins, and the Ravel family. As stock-stars we also had Mr. and Mrs. James W. Wallack, engaged with the view of making strong combinations with their uncle, but somehow they wouldn't "combine" much, and the three could very seldom be brought into the cast of one play. It made but little difference, however, as, with the exception of a night or two of DON CAESAR DE BAZAN (a splendid performance!), Mr. Wallack this season played to very thin audiences, whether in connection with his nephew and niece or by himself.

The Keans returned to the St. Charles in the spring, but, in consequence of Mrs. Kean being taken ill, the engagement was shortened to about a week. Mr. Kean offered to make a compensation for necessarily cutting the engagement down to seven nights, but I wouldn't listen to such a proposition. Nevertheless, he left a hundred dollars in the treasury out of the proceeds of his benefit, at which Mrs. Kean was not able to assist.

This season was so prosperous (even Mobile didn't turn out so badly as it usually had) that it was decided to refit and remodel the St. Charles at an estimated cost of $8000, which (of course) went up to $16,000.

The American Theatre on Poydras Street had been opened every season in some form or other, generally collapsing in the middle of winter, and throwing large numbers of people out of employment. This season it was conducted by Messrs. S.P. Stickney and Lucius Place (R.L. Place as his agent) as a theatre and circus, and had escaped the usual collapse.

A "combination" was formed for conducting the ensuing season of the St. Charles, American, and Mobile theatres under one management; that is to say, a board of directors was created, consisting of our firm and Stickney, by which all important matters were to be arranged, and the manager of each theatre to carry out the details. By virtue of our having two theatres to Stickney's one, we had two votes, being two thirds of the whole board; consequently, as my partner was the manager in Mobile, where he resided, the real weight of the management of all three theatres fell upon me. But the yoke was easy and the burden was light, as will be seen presently.

During this season, finding the houses sometimes affected by people staying away to hear expected news from Mexico, I adopted the plan of announcing from the stage any new tidings that might come in from the seat of war after the assemblage of the audience. Being on the best of terms with the editors of the Picayune (Kendall was with the army all through the war), I was enabled to obtain the very latest news during the evening, and it came to be understood that the St. Charles Theatre was the very best place for newsmongers to go to if they wanted to be posted up with the war proceedings on the Rio Grande. I remember announcing, on the 20th of March, the great victory of General Taylor over Santa Anna at Buena Vista on the 22d of the preceding month. When the applause and cheers had subsided, I added these words: "I prophesy that General Zachary Taylor will be the next President of the United States," when the applause and cheers were redoubled. I spoke as I thought, not as I wished. Henry Clay should have been elected the following year, but it seems that great and good man had to be thrust aside for "expediency."

On the 27th of February an actor of the American Theatre, by name Collins, departed this life. Attending his funeral on the 28th, it was found that the minister engaged to perform the funeral service could not attend. Being the senior actor present, I was requested to read the service, to which request I unhesitatingly assented, but there being no Liturgy at hand, I sent home for one, and we proceeded to the grave-yard, where my messenger met me with the book, and there I read the services for the burial of the dead according to the ritual of the New Jerusalem Church, all the actors and actresses present joining most devoutly in the ceremonies. . . .

A DINNER AT THE ST. CHARLES HOTEL
1846

The fame of New Orleans hospitality was epitomized in the appointments, service, and cuisine of the St. Charles Hotel. One of its most lavish epicurean dinners took place at seven o'clock on December 22, 1846. On the occasion of the annual dinner of the New England Club of the city, Henry Clay and Louisiana's governor, Isaac Johnson, were guests of honor. The Picayune reported that "ample justice was done to the dinner . . . and toasts were given . . . with hearty good feelings."

Source: New Orleans Daily Picayune, December 23, 1846.

SOUPS

Redfish Chowder
Clam Chowder

Mock Turtle Soup
Rice and Tomato Soup

FISH

Broiled Pompano, stewed sauce
Broiled Rockfish, Hollandaise do.
Codfish Tongues and Sounds

Redfish, Normandy fashion
Baked Redfish, larded, port wine sauce

BOILED

Turkies and oyster sauce
Buffalo Tongues
Beef Tongues
Corned Beef and Cabbage

Calf's Head and brain sauce
Leg of Mutton, caper sauce
Fulton Market Beef
Westphalia Hams cooked in Champagne

COLD AND ORNAMENTAL DISHES

Boned Turkies
Salmon Salads
Lobster Salads

Cold French Pies
Chicken Salads

BAKED

Pork and Beans
Oysters in the shell

Yankee Chicken Pies
Fried Oysters

ENTREES

Noix de Veau en Bedeau, sauce tomate
Tourband de Filets de Volaille
Colelettes de Mouton à la soubise

Riz de Veau aux épinards
Pigeons en compote
Timbales de Macaroni à la Milanaise
Canneton à la puree de pois verts
Croustades garnis de Becassines
Cotelettes de Veau, piques à la jardinière
Arcade de Volaille, garnis d'une Toulouse
Petits Bouchées à la Reine

ROASTS

Tenderloin of Beef, larded, plain sauce
Tenderloin of Beef, larded mushroom sauce
Turkies with Giblet gravy

Haunch of Venison, jelly sauce
Bear, apple sauce
Stuffed Capons
Pig

GAME

Mallard Ducks
Black Ducks
Teal Ducks

Canvass-back Ducks
Woodcocks   Wild Geese
Snipes   Brant

VEGETABLES

Green Peas, French fashion
Celery with brown gravy
Boiled Onions, plain sauce
Spinnage with cream
Croquettes of Potatoes
Turnips, butter sauce
Lettice with brown gravy

Carrots, stewed sauce
Cauliflower, plain sauce
Baked Cauliflower with cheese
Fried Parsnips
Baked mashed potatoes
Green Peas, boiled plain

PASTRY ORNAMENTS

Monument of St. George and the the Dragon
Sugar Vase with Kisses
Nougat Pyramid

Bunker Hill Monument
Chinese Light-House
Nougat Basket

PASTRY AND FRUIT

Charlotte Russe
Blanc Manger
Champagne Jelly
Oranges a la Belle Veu
Pumpkin Pies
Plum Puddings
Mine Pies
Vanilla Meringues

Parisian Gateaux
Lafayette Cakes
Citron Soufflage
Oranges   Grapes
Almonds   Figs
Raisins   Filberts
Pine Apples   Bananas
Apples   Pecans

Vanilla Ice Cream . . . Roman Punch . . . Coffee

WINES

Champagne
Claret
Hock

Madeira
Sherry
Port

A NEW YORKER VISITS NEW ORLEANS
1850

Some of the varied dimensions of the Ante-bellum New Orleans life have been preserved by the pen of travelers like Abraham Oakely Hall. Selections from this New Yorker's impressions of the city are an excellent example of how this travel literature can be useful to the student of the history of New Orleans.

Source: Abraham Oakely Hall, The Manhattener In New Orleans, Or Phases of Crescent City, New York, 1851.

Set the St. Charles Hotel down in St. Petersburg and you would think it a palace. In Boston, and ten to one you would christen it college. In London, and it would marvellously remind you of an exchange.

In New Orleans it is all three. A palace for creature comforts; a college for the study of human nature; and an exchange for money and appetite. But certainly, from the building's exterior, you would never imagine it a hotel unless waggishly told it was builded by Barnum, that immortal guardian of Tom Thumb, and American-godfather of Jenny Lind. And who, according to divers of the Connecticut people, is an intuitive architect. . . .

Imprimis, in the large bar room beneath the grand porch and reception hall, whose subterranean entrance from the pleasant air would impart great satisfaction to a regiment of Goughites, and add new spirits to their watery eloquence. For in it Emperor Appetite and King Alcohol hold their court in a most recherché style. There, of a winter's morning, when the sun is near meridian, or of a winter's evening, when the damp air or chilly northers without seem to say, "ah, apropos of sandwiches and punch," may be seen hundreds of steady, conscientious lovers of lunches and liquors going and returning, or clustering by pillar and column in social meriment, listening to the play of knife and fork and the click of spoons in heavy tumblers, and looking at the ruby sparkle in the polished decanters. Hungry men and those athirst getting new appetites. Those fresh from the gombo soup, and the ham, and the punch and julep, rushing back again, unable to be tormented by the mere looking on. Woe be to that deputy barkeeper, who in this retreat is slow of motion, or deficient in energy, or weak in constitution. I tremble to think of the juleps, and punches, and nogs, and soups, and plates of fish, and game, and beef and loaves of bread, that I have seen appear from side doors and vanish (like superior fireworks in old Niblo's of a dry week) among the waiting crowds at the long counter; or of the piles of dimes that each devoted (yet willing in all his agency) barkeeper swept into the little holes to nestle in boxes, and -- for aught you or I know, reader -- in barrels below. . . .

The Creole population of New Orleans possess one enjoyment well worth the envying -- an agreeable French opera! . . .

Entering from the street you are in a spacious lobby; the apperance of paint and flooring as fresh as those in Grammercy-Place Mansions; a jolly-looking citizen, whom you may see every day officiating with an amusing affectation of dignity as crier of a court, takes your tickets, and turns you over with your place-checks to the various <u>loge</u> directors, who bow you up or down, in and out, with a grace which, were you in England, or at the North, would suggest the possibility of there being an unappropriated quarter dollar in your miniature <u>porte-monnaie</u>. The parquet is already filled with critical young Creoles, and here and there a representative of "Young America," ambitious of connoisseur-ship in music; the well-brushed heads about, principally belong to scions of Creole aristocracy; family incomes, or salaries as genteel clerks, supplying the allowance of tri-weekly visits to the opera. Behind them, upon simple benches, are the unwashed patrons of Auber, Donizetti, and Halevy, who, for a dollar a head (less by a half the payments from the remainder of the audience) have left their ground-floor lodgings and red-curtained retreats, to gratify their love of harmony. . . .

America has given the world a printing press which is emblazoned in the History of Art. Who will next bid arise in her borders a Joint Stock Company for the publication of a newspaper, paying liberally for good gazette rhetoric, and so enrich the stockholders while benefitting society with a <u>good</u> newspaper?

It was the New Orleans Picayune newspaper which first gave a tone to the Crescent City press. In its infancy, it was an audacious little sheet; and when it came among its heavy-headed, half French, half naturalized compeers, created an impression some thing like that of a lively pin-wheel of a firework evening in the midst of some complicated assortment of powder and sulphur, bolstered up by a dozen hickory poles. It dared to joke with sugar, and to treat cotton as a light affair. It sneezed at tobacco, and waxed merry in the midst of tallow and ship chandlery. It wrote sonnets upon grave officials, who were accustomed to universal homage. Scarcely large enough to wrap around a loaf of bread, it was as full of witticisms as one of Thackeray's dreams after a light supper. It picked the locks of municipal portfolios, and sported with criminal justice. It taught the recorder that he was a born wit, and that the true way to enjoy his situation was to extract fun out of every prisoner arraigned. It woke up the captains of the police guard, and taught them to be funny. It ran with race-horses, and picked up all the good sayings on the turf. It lounged about the Levee, and hunted out rats and loafers with puns. In its office was a kaleidoscope, wherein every-day thoughts and every-day occurrences took new hues and curious combinations. . . .

THE CITY CHARTER OF 1852: PROVISIONS FOR FUNDING THE DEBT

One of the most important characteristics of this charter was its detailed description of a greatly increased city bureaucracy. Especially significant, however, are the stipulations regarding the management of the city debt.

Source: Revised Statutes of Louisiana, New Orleans, 1856.

SEC. 24. No money shall be drawn from the city treasury except the same shall have been previously appropriated for the purpose for which it was drawn.

SEC. 25. The Mayor shall have the qualifications required for members of the House of Representatives of the State; he shall keep his office in some central part of the city of New Orleans, which shall be determined by the Common Council; he shall have a seal, to be called the seal of the city of New Orleans, which shall be affixed to all proper official acts of the corporation; he shall see that the laws and ordinances within the limits of the city of New Orleans be properly executed; he shall be ex-officio justice and conservator of the peace; he, together with the Recorders of the city of New Orleans, shall be and compose a Police Board, a majority of whom shall act, and who shall make and confirm all police appointments, to-wit:

The Chief of Police should they in their judgment deem such office necessary; the captains, lieutenants, corporals and policemen of each district of the city; the wardens, under-wardens and employees of the work-houses, the superintendent, warden or keepers and employees of the district and city prisons, houses of refuge, and keepers or commissaries of the markets, and all other officers and men now appointed or nominated by the Mayor and confirmed or approved by the Common Council.

Said Police Board may suspend, remove or discharge all such officers, men and employees, for cause, and shall decide on all police matters pertaining to appointments, dismissals or grievances of or against the police, finally and without appeal. But the Mayor, or any one of the said Recorders, shall have the right temporarily to suspend until the next meeting of the Board thereafter, all persons employed in the police.

The meetings of the Board of Police mentioned above shall be public, and holden at the Mayor's office; all votes upon any subject or appointment shall be viva voce, and a correct record of all the proceedings of said Board shall be kept by the Secretary of the Mayor, and the proceedings of every meeting of said Board shall be published in the official journal of the city.

All appointments herein provided for by said Police Board shall be made in the month of April, one thousand eight hundred and fifty-three, by the Mayor and Recorders now elected, and such appointees shall qualify themselves by bond and oath of office, as may be provided for by existing laws, and enter upon the discharge of their duties on the first Monday of May next, until which time, and no longer, the present incumbents shall continue in office.

And thereafter, within ten days after the election and qualification of the Mayor and Recorders of the city, as provided for by law, the Police Board, composed as aforesaid, shall make and confirm all appointments, and said appointees shall enter upon the discharge of their duties, having first qualified themselves according to law, on the first of May following, and shall hold their offices respectively for a term of one year, unless sooner removed by the Police Board.

SEC. 29. The Comptroller shall have a general superintendence of the fiscal affairs of the Corporation. He shall prescribe the mode and form of keeping the Corporation books and accounts in every department entrusted with the receipt and expenditure of money; and the books and accounts shall at all times be subject to inspection. He shall examine and audit all claims and demands against or in favor of the Corporation.

No money shall be received by the Treasurer, or any other officer, from any source whatever, except on a written order, receipt or other document, signed by the Comptroller.

All accounts for collection of the revenue shall originate in his office. No money shall be paid out of the treasury, unless authorized by an ordinance or resolution of the Council, and on warrant signed by the Comptroller. He shall keep a full set of books, in which all the fiscal operations of the corporation shall be recorded. He shall, in the month of January of each year, lay before the Council a report of the receipts and expenditures during the past year, giving not only the various items of the receipts and expenditures, but a full detail of the names of all persons to whom money has been paid or notes or bonds issued, the amount thereof, the number of the warrant and date of the resolution or ordinance authorizing the expenditure.

The report shall also embrace a statement of the indebtedness of the city, showing, in detail, all outstanding obligations, their date, amount, to whom and for what issued, when due, and under what resolution or ordinance authorized. It shall also contain estimates of the receipts and expenditures for the current year, and in general, all such matter, in connection with the fiscal affairs of the city as the Comptroller may consider of public interest. Said report, in a condensed form, shall be published in the official paper; and such number of copies of the detailed report as the Council may direct shall be published in book form. All contracts for public works, or for materials or supplies ordered by the Council, shall be offered by the Comptroller at public auction, and given to the lowest bidder, who can furnish security satisfactory to the Council; provided the Council shall have the right to reject all bids.

THE GREAT YELLOW FEVER EPIDEMIC OF 1853

George W. Cable (1844-1925), the author of the selection below, gained international recognition for his critical novels and stories based on New Orleans and Louisiana Creole life. Having lived the first forty years of his life in New Orleans, one can sense in his description of the epidemic his intimate acquaintance with the city and its suffering.

George Washington Cable, The Creoles of Louisiana, New York, 1884.

Three-quarters of a century had passed over the little Franco-Spanish town, hidden under the Mississippi's downward-retreating bank in the edge of its Delta swamp on Orleans Island, before the sallow spectre of yellow fever was distinctly recognized in her streets and in her darkened chambers.

That it had come and gone earlier, but unidentified, is altogether likely. In 1766 especially, the year in which Ulloa came with his handful of Havanese soldiers to take possession for Spain, there was an epidemic which at least resembled the great West Indian scourge. Under the commercial concessions that followed, the town expanded into a brisk port. Trade with the West Indies grew, and in 1796, the yellow fever was confronted and called by name.

From that date it appeared frequently if not yearly, and between that date and the present day twenty-four lighter and thirteen violent epidemics have marked its visitations. At their own horrid caprice they came and went. In 1821, a quarantine of some sort was established, and it was continued until 1825; but it did not keep out the plague, and it was then abandoned for more than thirty years. Between 1837 and 1843, fifty-five hundred deaths occurred from the fever. In the summer and fall of 1847, over twenty-eight hundred people perished by it. In the second half of 1848, eight hundred and seventy-two were its victims. It had barely disappeared when cholera entered again and carried off forty-one hundred. A month after its disappearnce, -- in August, 1849, -- the fever returned; and when, at the end of November, it had destroyed seven hundred and forty-four persons, the cholera once more appeared; and by the end of 1850 had added eighteen hundred and fifty-one to the long rolls.

In the very midst of these visitations, it was the confident conviction and constant assertion of the average New Orleans citizen, Creole or American, on his levee, in the St. Charles rotunda, at his counting-room desk, in the columns of his newspaper, and in his family circle, that his town was one of the healthiest in the world. The fatality of the epidemics was principally among the unacclimated. He was not insensible to their sufferings, he was famous for his care of the sick: the town was dotted with orphan asylums. But in this far-away corner crucial comparisons escaped him. The Creole did not readily take the fever, and, taking it, commonly recovered. He had, and largely retains still, an absurd belief in his entire immunity from attack. When he has it, it is something else. As for strangers, -- he threw up his palms and eyebrows, -- nobody asked them to come to New Orleans. The mind of the American turned only to commerce; and the commercial value of a well-authenticated low death-rate he totally overlooked. Every summer might bring plague -- granted ; but winter brought trade, wealth. It thundered and tumbled through the streets like a surf. The part of a good citizen seemed to be to shut his eyes tightly and drown comment and debate with loud assertions of the town's salubrity. . . .

As the year 1853 drew near, a climax of evil conditions seemed to be approached. The city became more dreadfully unclean than before. The scavenging was being tried on a contract system, and the "foul and nauseous steams" from gutters, alleys, and dark nooks became intolerable. In the merchants' interest Carondelet basin and canal were being once more dug out; the New Canal was being widened; gas and water mains were being extended; in the Fourth District, Jackson Street and St. Charles Avenue were being excavated for the road-beds of their railways. In the Third District, many small draining trenches were being dug.

On the 12th of March, the ship Augusta sailed from Bremen for New Orleans with upward of two hundred emigrants. Thirteen days afterward the Northampton left Liverpool, bound in the same direction, with between three and four hundred Irish. She had sickness on board during the voyage, and some deaths. The Augusta had none. While these were on their way, the bark Siri, in the port of Rio de Janeiro, lost her captain and several of her crew by yellow fever, and afterward sailed for New Orleans. The ship Camboden Castle cleared from Kingston, Jamaica, for the same port, leaving seven of her crew dead of the fever. . . .

But suddenly the contagion leaped into the midst of the people. In the single week ending July 16th, two hundred and four persons were carried to the cemeteries. A panic seized the town. Everywhere porters were tossing trunks into wagons, carriages rattling over the stones and whirling out across the broad white levee to the steamboats' sides. Foot-passengers were hurrying along the sidewalk, luggage and children in hand, and out of breath, many a one with the plague already in his pulse. The fleeing crowd was numbered by thousands.

During the following week, the charity hospital alone received from sixty to one hundred patients a day. Its floors were covered with the sick. From the 16th to the 23d, the deaths averaged sixty-one a day. Presently, the average ran up to seventy-nine. The rains continued, with much lightning and thunder. The weather became tropical; the sun was scorching hot and the shade chilly. The streets became heavy with mud, the air stifling with bad odors, and the whole town a perfect Constantinople for foulness.

August came on. The week ending the 6th showed one hundred and eighty-seven deaths from other diseases, an enormous death-rate, to which the fever added nine hundred and forty-seven victims. For a week, the deaths in the charity hospital -- where the poor immigrants lay -- had been one every half hour.

The next day two hundred and twenty-eight persons died. The pestilence had attacked the Creoles and the blacks. In every direction were confusion, fright, flight, calls for aid, the good "Howards" hurrying from door to door, widows and orphans weeping, till the city was, as an eye-witness says, a "theatre of horrors."

"Alas," cried one of the city journals, "we have not even grave-diggers!" Five dollars an hour failed to hire enough of them. Some of the dead went to the tomb still with pomp and martial honors; but the city scavengers, too, with their carts, went knocking from house to house asking if there were any to be buried. Long rows of coffins were laid in furrows scarce two feet deep, and hurriedly covered with a few shovelfulls of earth, which the daily rains washed away, and the whole mass was left, "filling the air far and near with the most intolerable pestilential odors." Around the grave-yards funeral trains jostled and quarrelled for place, in an air reeking with the effluvia of the earlier dead. Many "fell to work and buried their own dead." Many sick died in carriages and carts. Many were found dead in their beds, in stores, in the streets. Vice and crime broke out fiercely: the police were never so busy. Heroism, too, was seen on every hand. Hundreds toiled for the comfort of sick and dying, and hundreds fell victims to their own noble self-abnegation. Forty-five distant cities and towns sent relief.

In the cemeteries of New Orleans, between the 1st of June and the 1st of October, nearly eleven thousand persons were buried. To these must be added the many buried without certificate, the hundreds who perished in their flight, and the multitudes who fell in the towns to which the pestilence was carried. It lingered through autumn, and disappeared only in December. During the year 1853 nearly thirty thousand residents of New Orleans were ill of the yellow fever, and there died, from all causes, nearly sixteen thousand.

In the next two summers, 1854 and '55, the fever returned and destroyed more than five thousand persons. Cholera added seventeen hundred and fifty. The two years' death-rates were seventy-two and seventy-three per thousand. That of 1853 was one hundred and eleven. In three years, thirty-seven thousand people had died, and wherever, by ordinary rate of mortality, there should have been one grave or sepulchre, there were four. One can but draw a sigh of relief in the assurance that this is a history of the past, not the present, and that new conditions have made it next to impossible that it should ever be repeated in the future. . . .

THE WILL OF JUDAH TOURO, NEW ORLEANS PHILANTHROPIST
1854

Judah Touro (1775-1854) was a self-made merchant who gave liberally to numerous charities in his adopted city and elsewhere. The Touro Infirmary and the Touro Synagogue were outstanding landmarks of New Orleans. This segment of his will reveals the complexity of Touro's interests and philanthropies.

Source: David C. Adelman, Esq., Life and Times of Judah Touro, New Orleans, 1936.

WILL OF JUDAH TOURO
UNITED STATES OF AMERICA,
STATE OF LOUISIANA,
CITY OF NEW ORLEANS

United States of America,
State of Louisiana, City of New Orleans

Be it known that on this sixth day of January, in the year of our Lord eighteen hundred and fifty-four, and of the independence of the United States of America the seventy-eighth, at a quarter before 10 o'clock a.m.,

Before me, Thomas Layton, a Notary Public, in and for the city of New Orleans aforesaid, duly commissioned and sworn, and in presence of Messrs. Jonathan Montgomery, Henry Shepherd, Jr., and George Washington Lee, competent witnesses, residing in said city, and hereto expressly required --

Personally appeared Mr. Judah Touro, of this city, merchant, whom I, the said Notary, and said witnesses, found sitting in a room, at his residence, No. 128 Canal Street, sick of body, but sound in mind, memory, and judgment, as did appear to me, the said Notary, and to said witnesses. And the said Mr. Judah Touro requested me, the Notary, to receive his last will or testament, which he dictated to me, Notary, as follows, to wit, and in presence of said witnesses:

1. I declare that I have no forced heirs.
2. I desire that my mortal remains be buried in the Jewish Cemetery in Newport, Rhode Island, as soon as practicable after my decease.
3. I nominate and appoint my trusty and esteemed friends Rezin Davis Shepherd of Virginia, Aaron Keppell Josephs of New Orleans, Gershom Kursheedt of New Orleans, and Pierre Andre Destrac Cazenave of New Orleans, my testamentary executors, and the detainers of my estate, making,

however, the following distinction between my said executors, to wit: To the said Aaron Keppell Josephs, Gershom Kursheedt, and Pierre Andre Destrac Cazenave, I give and bequeath to each one separately, the sum of ten thousand dollars, which legacies I intend respectively, not only as tokens of remembrance of those esteemed friends, but also as in consideration of all services they may have hitherto, rendered me, and in lieu of the commissions to which they would be entitled hereafter in the capacity of Testamentary Executors as aforesaid. And as regards my other designated executor, say my dear, old and devoted friend, Rezin Davis Shepherd, to whom, under Divine Providence, I was greatly indebted for the preservation of my life when I was wounded on the 1st of January, 1815, I hereby appoint and institute him, the said Rezin Davis Shepherd, after the payment of my particular legacies and the debts of my succession, the universal legatee of the rest and residue of my estate, movable and immovable.

In case of the death, absence or inability to act of one or more of my said Executors, I hereby empower the remaining Executor or Executors to act in carrying out the provisions of this my last will; and in the event of the death or default, of any one or more of my said Executors before my own demise, then in that case, it is my intention that the heirs or legal representatives of those who may depart this life before my own death, shall inherit in their stead the legacies herein above respectfully made to them.

4. I desire that all leases of my property and which may be in force at the time of my demise, shall be faithfully executed until the same shall have expired.

5. I desire that all the estate, real, personal and mixed, of which I may die possessed, shall be disposed of in the manner directed by this my last will or testament.

6. I give and bequeath to the Hebrew Congregation the "Dispersed of Judah" of the City of New Orleans, all that certain property situated in Bourbon Street, immediately adjoining their Synagogue, being the present schoolhouse, and the residence of the said Mr. Gershom Kursheedt, the same purchased by me from the bank of Louisiana; and also to the said Hebrew Congregation, the two adjoining brick houses purchased from the heirs of David Urquhart, the revenue of said property to be applied to the founding and support of the Hebrew school connected with said Congregation, as well as to the defraying of the salary of their Reader or Minister, said property to be conveyed accordingly by my said executors to said Congregation with all necessary restrictions.

7. I give and bequeath to found the Hebrew Hospital of New Orleans the entire property purchased for me, at the succession sale of the late C. Paulding, upon which property the building now known as the "Touro Infirmary" is situated; the said contemplated Hospital to be organized according to law, as a charitable institution for the relief of the indigent sick, by my executors and such other persons as they may associate with them conformably with the laws of Louisiana.

8. I give and bequeath to the Hebrew Benevolent Association of New Orleans five thousand dollars.

9. I give and bequeath to the Hebrew Congregation "Shangarai Chassed" of New Orleans five thousand dollars.

10. I give and bequeath to the Ladies' Benevolent Society of New Orleans, the sum of five thousand dollars.

11. I give and bequeath to the Hebrew Foreign Mission Society of New Orleans, five thousand dollars.

12. I give and bequeath to the Orphans' Home Asylum of New Orleans, the sum of five thousand dollars.

13. I give and bequeath to the Society for the relief of Destitute Orphan Boys in the Fourth District, five thousand dollars.

14. I give and bequeath to the St. Armas Asylum for the relief of destitute females and children, the sum of five thousand dollars.

15. I give and bequeath to the New Orleans Female Orphan Asylum, at the corner of Camp and Prytania streets, five thousand dollars.

16. I give and bequeath to the St. Mary's Catholic Boys' Asylum, of which my old and esteemed friend Mr. Anthony Rasch is chairman of its Executive Committee, the sum of five thousand dollars.

17. I give and bequeath to the Milne Asylum of New Orleans, five thousand dollars.

18. I give and bequeath to the "Firemen's Charitable Association" of New Orleans, five thousand dollars.

19. I give and bequeath to the "Seamen's Home," in the First District of New Orleans, five thousand dollars.

20. I give and bequeath, for the purpose of establishing an "Alms House" in the City of New Orleans, and with a view of contributing, as far as possible, to the prevention of mendicity in said city, the sum of eighty thousand dollars, (say $80,000) and I desire that the "Alms House" thus contemplated shall be organized according to law; and further, it may desire that after my executors shall have legally organized and established said contemplated Alms House, and appointed proper persons to administer and control the direction of its affairs, then such persons legally so appointed and their successors, in office, conjointly with the Mayor of the City of New Orleans, and his successors in office, shall have the perpetual direction and control thereof.

21. I give and bequeath to the City of Newport, in the State of Rhode Island, the sum of ten thousand dollars, on condition that the said sum be expended in the purchase and improvement of the property in said city, known as the "Old Stone Mill," to be kept as a public park or promenade ground.

22. I give and bequeath to the "Redwood Library" of Newport aforesaid, for books and repairs, three thousand dollars.

23. I give and bequeath to the Hebrew Congregation "Ohabay Shalome" of Boston, Massachusetts, five thousand dollars.

24. I give and bequeath to the Hebrew Congregation of Hartford, Connecticut, five thousand dollars.

25. I give and bequeath to the Hebrew Congregation of New Haven, Connecticut, five thousands dollars.

26. I give and bequeath to the North American Relief Society, for the Indigent Jews of Jerusalem, Palestine, of the City and State of New York (Sir Moses Montefiore of London, their agent), ten thousand dollars.

27. It being my earnest wish to co-operate with the said Sir Moses Montefiore of London, Great Britain, in endeavoring to ameliorate the condition of our unfortunate Jewish Brethren, in the Holy Land, and to secure to them the inestimable privilege of worshipping the Almighty according to our religion, without molestation, I therefore give and bequeath the sum of fifty thousand dollars, to be paid by my Executors for said object, through the said Sir Moses Montefiore, in such manner as he may advise, as best calculated to promote the aforesaid objects; and in case of any legal or other difficulty or impediment in the way of carrying said bequest into effect, according to my intentions, then and in that case, I desire that the said sum of fifty thousand dollars be invested by my Executors in the foundation of a Society in the City of New Orleans, similar in its objects to the "North American Relief Society for the Indigent Jews of Jerusalem, Palestine, of the City of New York," to which I have before referred in this my last will.

28. It is my wish and desire that the Institutions to which I have already alluded in making this will, as well as those to which in the further course of making this will, I shall refer, shall not be disqualified from inheriting my legacies to them respectively made, for reason of not being incorporated, and thereby not qualified to inherit by law; but on the contrary, I desire that the parties interested in such institutions and my executors shall facilitate their organization as soon after my decease as possible, and thus render them duly qualified by law to inherit in the premises according to my wishes.

29. I give and bequeath to the Jews' Hospital Society of the City and State of New York twenty thousand dollars.

30. I give and bequeath to the Hebrew Benevolent Society "Meshibat Nafesh" of New York, five thousand dollars. . . .

54. I give and bequeath to the three following Institutions, named in the will of my greatly beloved brother, the late Abraham Touro, of Boston, the following sums:

First, to the Asylum of Orphan Boys, in Boston, Massachusetts, five thousand dollars.

Second, to the Female Orphan Asylum of Boston aforesaid, five thousand dollars.

Third. And to the Massachusetts Female Hospital, ten thousand dollars.

55. I give and bequeath ten thousand dollars for the purpose of paying the salary of a Reader or Minister to officiate in the Jewish Synagogue of Newport, Rhode Island, and to endow the Ministry of the same, as well as to keep in repair and embellish the Jewish Cemetery in Newport aforesaid; the said amount to be appropriated and paid, or invested for that purpose in such manner as my executors may determine concurrently with the cor-

poration of Newport aforesaid, if necessary. And it is my wish and desire, that David Gould and Nathan H. Gould, sons of my esteemed friend the late Isaac Gould, Esq., of Newport aforesaid, should continue to oversee the improvements in said Cemetery and direct the same; and as a testimony of my regard and in consideration of services rendered by their said father, I give and bequeath the sum of two thousand dollars to be equally divided between them, the said David and said Nathan H. Gould. . . .

66. I revoke all other wills or testaments, which I may have made previously to these presents.

Thus, it was, that this testament or last will was dictated to me, the notary, by the said testator, in presence of the witnesses herein above named, and undersigned, and I have written the same, such as it was dictated to me, by the testator, in my own proper hand, in presence of said witnesses; and having read this testament in a loud and audible voice to the said testator, in presence of said witnesses, he, the said testator, declared in the same presence, that he well understood the same and persisted therein.

All of which was done at one time without interruption or turning aside to other acts.

Thus done and passed at the said City of New Orleans, at the said residence of the said Mr. Judah Touro, the day, month and year first before written in the presence of Messrs. Jonathan Montgomery, Henry Shepherd, Jr., and George Washington Lee, all three being the witnesses as aforesaid, who, with the said testator, and me, the said notary, have hereunto signed their names.

                            (Signed.)
                      J. TOURO,
                      J. MONTGOMERY,
                      H. SHEPHERD, JR.,
                      GEO. W. LEE,
                      THOS. LAYTON, <u>Notary Public</u>.

THE NEW ORLEANS MARDI GRAS BEGINS
1857

In the following items, the New Orleans newspaper L'Abeille (The Bee) described the ball and tableaux presented by the pioneer organization of the Mardi Gras in the city, the Mistick Krewe of Comus. Their theme for their two floats was "The Demon Actors in Milton's Paradise Lost."

Source: Perry Young, The Mistick Krewe: Chronicles of Comus and His Kin, New Orleans, 1931.

FROM L'ABEILLE (THE BEE)

Wednesday, Feb. 25, 1857:
   . . . The theatres and other places were finely attended, especially Crisp's Gaiety, where the "Mystick Krewe of Komus" gave a brilliant and peculiar entertainment in the nature of a ball, which, with their ceremonies in procession, passed off with great eclat. The novelty of their character may induce us to allude to them more fully tomorrow."

Thursday, Feb. 26, 1857:
   For what purpose the strange 'Krewe of Komus,' as they stylé themselves, have set their vessel at sail over a sea of mystical ceremonies, whence commenced their voyage, and whither are they bound, are questions to be answered only within the widest limits of vague conjecture.
   "A kurious kompanie of four skore or more seem to have set out from New Orleans on or about the 30th of December, 1856, to have krossed the lake to Mobile, and having reconnoitered that city on the first of January last, to have again set sail for this port with a rare cargo of mysticisms, kollected under the direction of a kritical superkargo, kurioso, supernumerary virtuoso of Komus, an island as yet unlocated and unnumbered in geographical and governmental nomenclature. Farther than this, and that the origin of this krewe must be recent, and probably as we have given it, we would not venture further speculation concerning an offspring whose mobile movements rather indicate a Mobile parentage. To lay aside the reticencies, this krewe is one who have chosen the 24th of February for a manifestation of some superb character in imitation of, or for the purpose of surpassing, some Mobilians in their strange way of celebrating New Year's day. Accordingly, they got up a characteristic ball at the Gaiety Theatre, with several tableaux of unsurpassed magnificence, to lend brilliancy to the occasion. The krewe was a strange, mixed, masked company, representing every variety of character and human peculiarities, from the "Drunk-

ard" up, through "Death" to the "Devil," with here and there a "Paul Pry," a "Pickpocket" or a "Cowbellan" passing in review in ludicruous procession before us.

"The tableaux witnesed, the masked mysticks were joined in mazy dances by as many persons as possible from the jammed audience, who kept up the gay festivities till early morn. Such things will serve for a twelve-month. . . .

GENERAL BUTLER TAKES COMMAND OF NEW ORLEANS
1862

After New Orleans fell to the Federal forces in March of 1862, General Benjamin Franklin Butler became military governor of the city. His command soon became a cause célèbre, because of the decisive actions he took to deal with a rebellious population. The following selection captures the drama of bitter confrontations of loyalties, as well as the realities encountered by the occupying forces.

Source: Nathan Weiss, "The Political Theory and Practice of General Benjamin Franklin Butler," Ph. D. New York University, 1961. Reprinted with permission of the author.

Always hard pressed to find a suitable post for the Massachusetts political general, those in authority finally decided to give Butler command of the operations to be directed against New Orleans. During March, 1862, after Farragut's fleet had neutralized the forts below New Orleans, Butler's forces occupied the city. It was as military governor of this surly and rebellious area that he was to be accorded much praise and abuse. His administration, as even his enemies admitted, was altogether fearless and, although ruthless, in many ways beneficial.

In New Orleans Butler set up his headquarters at the St. Charles Hotel. While he was conferring there with the city's officials, an unruly mob gathered outside the building. Soon one of his officers rushed in, his uniform in shreds, and informed the general that the crowd was getting out of hand. Thereupon, in Napoleonic tradition, Butler ordered one of his commanders to ". . . clear the streets at once with his artillery." Terrified, the city officials begged Butler to rescind his order. Relenting, he offered them a chance to calm the mob, but they were unable to do so. A cry now went up from the enraged crowd: "Where's old Butler? Let him show himself. Let him come out here if he dare." Immediately, in true melodramatic style, Butler, cap in hand, stepped to the balcony and bellowed: "Who calls me? I am here." A hush now fell over the mob. Suddenly a roar was heard in the distance and all turned to see what caused it. Their eyes were greeted by the sight of the Sixth Maine battery of six Napoleons thundering down the street with wheels bouncing high and sparks flying. Within a few minutes the entire square was empty.

Having cowed the city, Butler turned to the problem of administering the unruly populace. Many of his acts brought him both notoriety and hatred. One of the most outstanding of these was the Mumford affair. William B. Mumford, a sporting man and gambler, had, before Butler's arrival, hauled down the United States flag which flew over the United States Mint Building. Mumford tore the flag to bits and paraded around town with a strip of it in his coat lapel. When Butler heard of this he vowed to his officers: "I will hang that fellow whenever I catch him." In due time Mumford was caught and, despite the pleadings of his wife and many worthy citizens, he was hanged from a beam in front of the Mint in accordance with the Spanish custom of executing the criminal at the "scene of his crime."

Another of his actions which created a national and international furor was Butler's famous "Woman's Order." The Federals in the Gulf City were spat on, hissed at, and called names by the defiant women of the city. These wives and daughters of Southern aristocracy had developed the habit of turning their backs on the hated Yankees. This led Butler to remark sarcastically: "These women evidently know which end of them looks best." Finally, to put a stop to this form of female defiance, the General issued his famed General Order No. 28 which announced that any woman who should by word, gesture or movement insult or show contempt for a United States soldier would be treated as a woman of the streets plying her "trade." This action roused a storm of protest. "Beast Butler," rose the cry. A reward of ten thousand dollars was put on his head by a gentleman from Charleston. . . .

The potential characterization of New Orleans' lady patriots as "women of the town" was especially resented by the prostitutes. To revenge themselves, they acquired quantities of Butler's pictures and affixed them to the bottoms of their toilets. Upon learning of this, the General ordered his troops to destroy all equipment thus marked. . . .

FEDERAL RESPONSES TO THE MECHANICS INSTITUTE RACE RIOTS 1866

Bloody race riots occurred in front of the Mechanics Institute in the city on July 30, 1866. Such violence represented the white Southerner's deep bitterness and confusion after their defeat by the Union forces, and precipitated participation of blacks in constitutional changes which signalled the new society of Reconstruction. The reports on the riots below were communicated to the House of Representatives by President Andrew Johnson on a motion in that house requesting a full investigation.

Source: New Orleans Riots, Executive Document No. 28, The House of Representatives, 29th Congress, 2nd Session, Washington, D.C., January 29, 1867.

HEADQUARTERS ARMIES OF THE UNITED STATES
Washington, D.C., August 10, 1866

SIR: I have the honor to enclose to you mail copies of General Sheridan's despatches on the New Orleans riots, and to ask their publication in full. Already a garbled version of one of these despatches, and an incomplete copy of another, have appeared in the public prints. These publications put General Sheridan in the position of taken a partisan view of the whole question, and, what is still worse, of being one day on one side of the question and again on the other. His despatches given in full show that he takes no partisan view, but that he reports what he conceives to be the facts without regard to who is hit.

I am just in receipt of a despatch from General Sheridan showing displeasure at his despatches getting into print in a mutilated and incomplete form.

I have the honor to be, very respectfully, your obedient servant,
U.S. GRANT, General

Hon. E.M. STANTON, Secretary of War.

OFFICE UNITED STATES MILITARY TELEGRAPH
Headquarters, War Department

The following telegram received, 2 p.m. July 28, 1866, from New Orleans, July 28, 1866
President JOHNSON.

Radical mass meeting, composed mainly of large number of negroes, last night, ending in a riot. The committee of arrangements of said meeting assembling to-night. Violent and incendiary speeches made; negroes called to arm themselves; you bitterly denounced. Speakers: Field, Dostie, Hawkins, Henderson, Heirward, and others. Governor Wells arrived last night, but sides with the convention move. The whole matter before grand jury, but impossible to execute civil process without certainty of riot. Contemplated to have the members of the convention arrested under process from the criminal court of this district. Is the military to interfere to prevent process of court?

        ALBERT VOORHIES,
          Lieutenant Governor of Louisiana
        ANDREW J. HERRON,
          Attorney General of Louisiana

     [Telegram]
         EXECUTIVE MANSION
   Washington, D.C., July, 28, 1866 -- 5:40 p.m.

ALBERT VOORHIES,
 Lieutenant Governor of Louisiana, New Orleans, La.

The military will be expected to sustain, and not to obstruct or interfere with, the proceedings of the courts. A despatch on the subject of the convention was sent to Governor Wells this morning.

         ANDREW JOHNSON.

      CORONER'S REPORT

July 31, 1866. -- Charles Johnson, (colored,) 30 years, a pistol ball penetrating the peritoneum of the small intestine; James Nelson, (colored,) 28 years, a pistol ball penetrating the right lung, at the basis thereof; Collins Page, (colored,) 28 years, a pistol ball in the brain and two in the body; Constant Loup, (white,) 36 years, stabbed with a dirk or knife, causing a wound three inches in length, cutting the intestine of the liver; E.H. Cenas, (white,) 22 years, a pistol ball which cut the carotid artery on the right side.

August 1, 1866. -- Wilson Johnson, (colored,) 40 years, a pistol ball in the right lung, and several wounds inflicted on the head with a blunt instrument.

The foregoing is a list of the bodies on which I have made a separate inquest, while engaged at that duty. Notice was left at about 10 o'clock a.m. at my office, requiring me to proceed at once to the workhouse to make inquest on the bodies of twenty-two (22) negroes who were killed in the riot of July 30 last. My deputy, Mr. L. Burthe, without delay, complied, and found 22 bodes enclosed in coffins, around which a hot fire had been lit for protection against the arising stench and for purification of the air. Not a solitary person was found on the spot to identify the bodies; and, as it was of the utmost urgency to have the bodies removed, (as the workhouse contained a population of 450 persons,) my deputy was constrained to make a general inquest in the presence of a jury, who found that the 22 persons in question had come to death by pistol-shots and stabbings, done during the riot of July 30, 1866.

Your most obedient servant,

C.C. DELIRY, Coroner.

A true copy of original report of Surgeon Hartsuff:

LOUIS N. CAZIARC,
Brevet Captain and Aide-de-Camp.

Official copy:

E.D. TOWNSEND,
Assistant Adjutant General.

REPORT OF THE BOARD OF INVESTIGATION UPON THE NEW ORLEANS RIOTS.

The board, having maturely considered the foregoing evidence, would respectfully report as follows:

The immediate causes of this riot, which the board are directed to investigate, are, in their opinion, to be found in the violent feelings of hostility towards the so-called convention of 1864, which had for some time prevailed in the community, and which were finally, by the course of events, fanned into the flame of an actual outbreak of riot, bloodshed, and massacre.

The board do not consider themselves called upon to decide or discuss in any manner the question of the legal existence and powers of the convention as such. Whether any attempted official action on their part would have been recognized by the courts as of any legal validity is a point admitting of grave doubt. This, however, was not the question under discussion between the civil and military authorities, the decision of which was, as it appears, pregnant with the gravest of consequences to the State and the nation. That question was, whether the persons claiming to constitute such conventions should be allowed to assemble.

The board will endeavor to state, briefly and comprehensively, the action of the civil and military authorities upon this point, and will make a short comparison of testimony thereon, with a view of deciding the cause and fixing the responsibility for the non-arrival of the United States troops in time to prevent the bloodshed which took place. The events of the day will then be considered in chronological order, the board making the best summary in their power of the voluminous evidence which they have taken, and which, in their opinion, points with irresistible force to the quarter in which the accountability for crime will be found to rest.

In regard to the scenes which now took place around the building, and the manner in which the allied forces in the street conducted the siege, the board cannot undertake to present even a summary of the evidence. They can only say that the work of massacre was pursued with a cowardly ferocity unsurpassed in the annals of crime. The escaping negroes were mercilessly pursued, shot, beaten, and stabbed to death by mob and police. Wounded men on the ground begging for mercy were savagely despatched by mob, police, firemen, and, incredible as it may appear, in two instances by women, (pages 326, 330.) But in two or three most honorable and exceptional cases white men and members of the convention were protected by members of the police, both against the mob and against other policemen. The chief of police, by great exertions, defended in this manner Governor Hahn. After the attack had commenced the police appeared to be under no control as such, but acted as and with the mob. Their cheers and waving of hats as they threw the mangled Dostie, then supposed a corpse, like a dead dog into the cart, sufficiently show their unison of feeling with their allies, (pages 340, 243, 358.) It will appear from the evidence of an assistant editor of the New Orleans Times, that it was only by announcing his character as such that he saved himself from instant death at the hands of the police, (page 21.) A reporter of the same paper saved himself in a similar manner, but narrowly escaped subsequent maltreatment on suspicion of having worn crape for Lincoln. . . .

In conclusion, the board will state that it is by no means their opinion that hostility to northern and Union men so pervades the community at large, as of itself either to endanger either their life or property, provided they refrain from claiming freedom of speech concerning subjects on which, like that of slavery before the war, no difference of opinion is tolerated. But in regard to the party which elected Mayor Monroe, and which through him now controls in a great measure the municipal government and city police, this party the board do consider as most thoroughly imbued with the spirit of hostility alluded to, and so soon as the lapse of sufficient time shall have convinced them that no punishment is to be anticipated for past offences, and that they need be no longer "on their good behavior," then, in the board's opinion, a period of insecurity for northern life and property will recommence.

The recent success of this party at the polls is, in the board's opinion, due first to the fact that its candidate was peculiarly identified with the confederate cause; and secondly, to the unfortunate apathy of the best classes of the community on the subject of municipal elections, which appears to be the curse of large cities, and results in throwing the government thereof into unworthy hands.

The commission have thus endeavored to give as concisely as possible the conclusions at which they have been compelled to arrive on the subject of the causes of, and responsibility for, the recent bloodshed. What, if any, action is called for, is for the decision of higher authority.

SANITARY ORDINANCES OF NEW ORLEANS
JUNE 25, 1879

The following sanitary ordinances were succinct statements of hygienic practices of the time.

Source: Louisiana Board of Health, <u>Reports of 1879</u>, New Orleans, 1879.

AN ORDINANCE <u>for the better protection and presevation of the public health</u>.

SECTION 1. <u>Be it ordained by the Council of the City of New Orleans</u>, That no person shall bring or cause to be brought into the limits of the city of New Orleans any hides, bones, peltry, rags or other articles whatsoever which may tend to produce infection, or in any way to injure or endanger health.

SEC. 2. No person shall sell, or offer or expose for sale in public or private any blown stale, decaying, putrid, rotten, or unwholesome provisions, vegetables, fruits or tainted meats or fish or any impure or unsound food, or any drink liable to be injurious to health, or the flesh of any animal that has died of disease, or which was diseased when killed.

SEC. 8. The Administrator of Police shall upon complaint of the Board of Health, remove or cause to be removed any foul or offensive matters whatever, to such place or places as may be selected by said Board, at the expense of the owner of said matter, or the occupant or owner of the premises where the same may be.

SEC. 13. The Board of Health may, in its discretion, for the protection of life and health, declare any structure or place unhealthy, and may order such structure or place forthwith to be vacated and closed; and the same shall not again be occupied until it shall appear to have been so cleansed or repaired as to be fit for human habitation, and permission shall have been granted accordingly by the Board of Health.

SEC. 24. No tomb, grave or vault containing any dead body shall be opened without permission, in writing, from the proper officers of the Board of Health, and no human body or remains thereof, within the jurisdiction of said Board, shall be disinterred or disentombed without its written authority, or be removed from or brought within the limits of the city of New Orleans without such authority first obtained.

SEC. 25. Every sexton or other person having charge of any cemetery, graveyard or burying ground shall, on Monday of each week, before the hour of 9 A.M., make a written report and hand the same into the office of the Board of Health; which said report shall contain the full name of each and every person buried in such cemetery, yard or ground during the seven days next preceding 6 o'clock P.M. of the last Sunday before making such report, together with a statement of the color, sex, age, nativity, the cause of death of such person, occupation, place of death, social condition and birth place of parents; also what interments were made in the ground and what interments in vaults or tombs, together with the numbers and owners of said vaults or tombs and such other information as the Board of Health may from time to time require.

SEC. 26. The Board of Health may remove or cause to be removed to hospital or other place of treatment any person or persons suffering from small-pox whenever such removal shall, in the discretion of said board, be deemed necessary for the proper treatment of such person or persons for the prevention or spread of said disease.

SEC. 27. All practitioners of medicine masters of any water-craft, hotel, boarding or lodging-house keepers, principals or masters of any public or private school, the chief officers or persons in charge of any public institution of charity or of punishment, and heads of families are hereby required to report, within twenty-four hours, to the office of the Board of Health all cases within their cognizance of Asiatic cholera, leprosy, Yellow Fever, typhus or ship fever, diptheria, malignant scarlet fever, small-pox, varioloid, trichiniasis, or any other case that may at any time be specified by the Board of Health.

SEC. 28. Parents shall inform principals of schools attended by their children of any contagious disease occurring in their families.

SEC. 29. All animals sick with any contagious or infectious disease shall be removed at once beyond the limits of the city of New Orleans by the person or persons owning or having charge of said animals, and in default of such action said animals may be removed by the Board of Health at the expense of such person or persons.

SEC. 33. All citizens are hereby authorized to lodge complaints at the office of the Board of Health, or with the sanitary inspectors, or with the sanitary police officers, of any violation of this ordinance; and in order to facilitate such complaints, books of complaint shall be kept at the office of the Board of Health, and at the office of each sanitary inspector, and said books shall be at all times open for entering therein any complaint or wrong.

SEC. 34. No person shall willfully obstruct, hinder or resist any officer or person, duly authorized by the Board of Health, in the execution or enforcement of any sanitary ordinance or order of said board, or in entering into or upon any premises for the purpose of examining the same.

SEC. 35. The penalty for violation of any section or portion of this ordinance shall be a fine not exceeding twenty-five dollars, recoverable before the recorder of the district wherein the offense was committed; or in default of payment of the fine, imprisonment not exceeding thirty days for each and every offense.

SEC. 37. That the members of the Board of Health and its agents, officers and employes, and the members of the Crescent City Police and the Recorders of the several districts of this city are specially charged with the enforcement of the provisions of this ordinance. . . .

REPORT ON THE SANITARY CONDITIONS OF THE CITY
1882

The constant threat of epidemics in New Orleans placed a great responsibility upon the sanitary inspectors of the city. The following selection describes the actual conditions in the city for 1882.

Source: Louisiana Board of Health, <u>Reports of 1882</u>, New Orleans, 1882.

DRAINAGE.

Although this district now constitutes the center of the business and enterprise in this city, the system of drainage is as primitive as of old. Surface drainage still prevails, and very imperfect it is at its best. After heavy rain storms, it is a common sight to see the rear of the district under water, which even extends as far front as Magazine street. The drainage machines have to labor for days before this surplus of water is carried off.

There is a fall in the surface slope of some fourteen or fifteen feet to the low lands, three miles distant from the river. The canals leading into the lake are on a highar level than the lands adjoining, from which the drainage machines are necessary to raise the rain water into these conduits.

SANITARY CONDITIONS.

The front of the district, as far back as Rampart street, is, generally speaking, in a fair sanitary condition the whole year. This is owning to the streets being paved, with some exceptions, and the gutters in consequence are capable of carrying off drainage waters. This is facilitated by the Camp street culvert and the Melpomene street canal.

The rear of the district is given over to mud. The street railways, on Clio and Erato streets, have improved the streets by planking, which is vastly superior to <u>mud</u>. The extreme rear of the district being so low and so often overflowed either by rain or lake waters, besides being traversed by the sewerage canals, is the least desirable for habitation. This is so on Canal street. This portion of the city, however, will never build up until an entirely new system of drainage is perfected and carried into operation. The city, in fact, will never build out to the lake, and become then the Southern Metropolis, so often prophesized, until this is done. The drainage into the lake is wrong in every way. The river and not the lake should receive the sewerage of the city.

HEALTH.

The past year was remarkably healthy for the entire city. The summer was cool, and the fall a late and pleasant ending of the warm season.

The mortality was light in this district, with its aggregate population of fully sixty thousand persons. The deaths from all causes gave a ratio per 1000 per annum of 31.85 white, 58.05 colored, and 38.31 total. This embraces the mortality in the Charity Hospital, an institution that receives its patients from all parts of the State and country, which had a death list of 510 whites, 294 colored, and 804 total. If this was deducted from the death rate given above, the ratio would be as follows: Whites, 15.16; colored, 37.23; total, 19.51 -- a reduction of almost one-half in the percentage of deaths.

The deaths were light for every month in the year, except April, May, June, November and December. The maximum was reached in December, and the minimum in August.

The mortality from malarial fevers was greatest in June and November. Typhoid fever, never common in this city, was the cause of twenty-four deaths, most of which occurred in the Charity Hospital. The absence of this fever to a great extent in this city is in favor of surface drainage.

The prevalence of contagious diseases was confined principally to scarlet fever and small-pox, but particularly the latter. Small-pox was mostly in the lower districts last winter and spring, but bids fair to extend on up through the upper ones this year. From present appearances, however, I would consider that its spread will be slow. This will be the case probably if the remainder of the winter should be mild and the spring an early one. The disease seems to be at a stand-still in this district at present, there being but four cases on hand. About seventy-five per cent of the cases occur among the colored race. The death-rate in this disease is very high, fully fifty per cent of the cases resulting fatally.

There is a total disregard of the merits of vaccination on the part of both whites and blacks in the lower classes. Gratuitous vaccination is repeatedly proffered to persons in the infected localities, but very seldom accepted. . . .

SANITATION.

Owing to the inadequacy of the force in this district, it has been impossible to accomplish as much in this direction as was necessary to materially improve the sanitary condition of premises, both public and private. The size of the district calls for at least three sanitary policemen, who have to inspect, look after contagious diseases, and attend to complaints. Two men, the present force, cannot go over the entire district between the first of the year and the beginning of summer, the time in which it ought to be done; in fact, the force cannot do it in twelve months at all satisfactorily.

The summer passing without the appearance of a case of yellow fever in this district, it was happily unnecessary to repeat the operations of the preceding years, in distributing disinfectants from house to house, etc., in anticipation of its spread. In the month of July, however, the entire front of the district, from the river back to Camp street, was inspected and disinfected as a matter of precaution. By means of a cart, procured from the City Hall, the officers were enabled to carry their disinfectants to all the premises for distribution. Instead of leaving the disinfectants at the houses, with instructions how to dissolve them, etc., given to the inmates, as was done by the Sanitary Association's force, the officers saw to the disinfection of the vaults themselves. The carts of the Association hauled the rubbish and garbage away that were cleaned out by the laboring men, who worked under the supervision of my officers.

BAKERIES.

These establishments were visited in November, and careful inquiry and examination made as to the kind of water used in making bread. The majority of them were found to depend mainly or altogether on river water, which is allowed to stand a sufficient time for the deposit of the sand and earthy matters before using. The remaining ones, with two or three exceptions, claimed to use cistern water, but had to resort to well water, in a measure, during the drouth. The exceptions, which parties will be looked after, admitted that they preferred well water, as it made lighter and better bread. Whether this assertion is true or not is a question.

MANUFACTORIES, PUBLIC BUILDINGS, ETC.

The majority of these buildings are in this district. The attention paid to them in the years has been principally that of enforcing their sanitary cleanliness. Quite a number of them make use of large iron tanks, holding from 1000 to 2000 gallons, as receptacles for excrementitious matters. The manufactories, where so many persons are employed, have the largest of them. The necessity for the cleaning of these vaults at short intervals is imperative. At least once a month is not too often. The vault of the St. James Hotel, so long complained of, has been thoroughly repaired. The same may be said of the vaults of the Recorder's and Criminal Court Buildings. The breweries and soap works in the district are in good sanitary condition; also, the sugar refineries. There are hide-stores and tanneries, in front of the district, which are somewhat nuisances in their way. This must be particularly so in the summer. I would recommend some action in this matter.

MARKETS.

The public markets are visited every week or ten days, and notice is taken of their sanitary condition at each inspection. The most trouble is with the Poydras and St. Mary's markets, but especially the former. The Poydras Market, as I am reliably informed, has not been properly washed out for the past two or three months. It is not quite so bad with St. Mary's Market. The fault lies with the lessees of these markets, who are directly violating the ordinance bearing on markets. There is no fault to find with the Dryades Market which is kept in excellent condition.

The private markets, somewhat scattered in this district, were also inspected during the year. They are usually kept in good order.

PUBLIC SCHOOLS.

These schools were carefully examined by my predecessor, Dr. Joseph Holt, in the fall of 1881. I found no trouble, therefore, in visiting them myself. I was shown a register by the principal of a school at once, where the names of scholars having certificates of vaccination were entered. This was so in all the white schools. The principals of the Fisk schools (colored) for boys and for girls, separate, had not been particular in this respect. About two-thirds of the pupils were known to have received certificates the year before. My visit to these schools was just before the holidays, and I did not have time to begin examining the scholars that were considered doubtful. This will be done, however, as soon as the schools open in January.

The vaults of the Fisk schools were found in a very leaky condition, and the urinals in the boys' school in need of repairs. The basement room in the girls' department for the primary scholars can only be used when it is dry and warm; at other times the principal, Mrs. Williams, has to dismiss them. The vaults of a number of the white schools required cleaning, and notices have been served on the school board for that purpose.

The building now known as the Garfield school was formerly used as a school of medicine, and of course is unsuited for its present purpose. This is only temporary, however, until the new McDonogh No. 13 school is ready for occupation.

I must plead in behalf of Mrs. M. Stamps, the estimable Principal of the New Orleans Central High School for Girls, for an early change in the present year to a building better adapted for school purposes and in a more desirable locality. This building was originally occupied as a colored school, and selected by the School Board as a substitute for the building on Calliope, now the University of Louisiana for the Colored Race, some time last winter. This school is on a key lot, and the back portion of the houses surrounding, on the block, abut against the grounds as in a circle. The odors emanating naturally from these buildings are sometimes so powerful that, as I was informed, the teachers and scholars are obliged to go to the front of the school building, facing on Clio street, to escape the effluvia. Besides, there are two rooms out of the five that are badly ventialted and poorly supplied with light. As a High School for Girls, every comfort and convenience to the teachers and scholars should be considered in connection therewith.

I have no fault to find with the other schools in particular. Generally speaking, they are very good schools indeed. In course of time there is no doubt that only such buildings as those known as the McDonough Schools will be in use in this city for educational purposes. . . .

MARK TWAIN ARRIVES IN NEW ORLEANS
1883

Aside from the salty wit and sureness of eye that one expected of Mark Twain, his impressions of New Orleans revealed the same genuine amazement that he experienced when visiting the cities of Europe. These selections give some of Twain's "Alladin's lamp experiences" in the "metropolis of the South."

Source: Mark Twain, Life on the Mississippi, Boston, 1883.

    The approaches to New Orleans were familiar; general aspects were unchanged. When one goes flying through London along a railway propped in the air on tall arches, he may inspect miles of upper bedrooms through the open windows, but the lower half of the houses is under his level and out of sight. Similarly, in high-river stage, in the New Orleans region, the water is up to the top of the enclosing levee-rim, the flat country behind it lies low -- representing the bottom of a dish -- and as the boat swims along, high on the flood, one looks down upon the houses and into the upper windows. There is nothing but that frail breastwork of earth between the people and destruction.
    The old brick salt-warehouses clustered at the upper end of the city looked as they had always looked; warehouses which had had a kind of Aladdin's lamp experience, however, since I had seen them; for when the war broke out the proprietor went to bed one night leaving them packed with thousands of sacks of vulgar salt, worth a couple of dollars a sack, and got up in the morning and found his mountain of salt turned into a mountain of gold, so to speak, so suddenly and to so dizzy a height had the war news sent up the price of the article.
    The vast reach of plank wharves remained unchanged, and there were as many ships as ever; but the long array of steamboats had vanished; not altogether, of course, but not much of it was left.
    The city itself had not changed -- to the eye. It had greatly increased in spread and population, but the look of the town was not altered. The dust, waste-paper-littered, was still deep in the streets; the deep, trough-like gutters alongside the curb-stones were still half full of reposeful water with a dusty surface; the sidewalks were still -- in the sugar and bacon region -- incumbered by casks and barrels and hogsheads; the great blocks of austerely plain commercial houses were as dusty-looking as ever.
    Canal Street was finer, and more attractive and stirring than formerly,

with its drifting crowds of people, its several processions of hurrying street-cars, and -- toward evening -- its broad second-story verandas crowded with gentlemen and ladies clothed according to the latest mode.

Not that there is any "architecture" in Canal Street: to speak in broad, general terms, there is no architecture in New Orleans, except in the cemeteries. It seems a strange thing to say of a wealthy, far-seeing, and energetic city of a quarter of a million inhabitants, but it is true. There is a huge granite U.S. Custom-house -- costly enough, genuine enough, but as a decoration it is inferior to a gasometer. It looks like a state prison. But it was built before the war. Architecture in America may be said to have been born since the war. New Orleans, I believe, has had the good luck -- and in a sense the bad luck -- to have had no great fire in late years. It must be so. If the opposite had been the case, I think one would be able to tell the "burnt district" by the radical improvement in its architecture over the old forms. One can do this in Boston and Chicago. The "burnt district" of Boston was commonplace before the fire; but now there is no commerical district in any city in the world that can surpass it -- or perhaps even rival it -- in beauty, elegance, and tastefulness.

However, New Orleans has begun -- just this moment, as one may say. When completed, the new Cotton Exchange will be a stately and beautiful building; massive, substantial, full of architectural graces; no shams or false pretences or uglinesses about it anywhere. To the city, it will be worth many times its cost, for it will breed its species. What has been lacking hitherto, was a model to build toward; something to educate eye and taste; a suggester, so to speak.

The city is well outfitted with progressive men -- thinking, sagacious, long-headed men. The contrast between the spirit of the city and the city's architecture is like the contrast between waking and sleep. Apparently there is a "boom" in everything but that one dead feature. The water in the gutters used to be stagnant and slimy, and a potent disease-breeder; but the gutters are flushed now, two or three times a day, by powerful machinery; in many of the gutters the water never stands still, but has a steady current. Other sanitary improvements have been made; and with such effect that New Orleans claims to be (during the long intervals between the occasional yellow-fever assaults) one of the healthiest cities in the Union. There's plenty of ice now for everybody, manufactured in the town. It is a driving place commercially, and has a great river, ocean, and railway business. At the date of our visit, it was the best lighted city in the Union, electrically speaking. The New Orleans electric lights were more numerous than those of New York, and very much better. One had this modified noonday not only in Canal and some neighboring chief streets, but all along a stretch of five miles of river frontage. There are good clubs in the city now -- several of them but recently organized -- and inviting modern-style pleasure resorts at West End and Spanish Fort. . . .

BUSINESS "BOOSTERS"
1894

"Booster" books and pamphlets played a large role in the development of the American city. By trumpeting the unique advantages of their business community, new investors, cheap migrant labor, or new customers might be attracted to the city. A particularly good example of such municipal public relations was the following rosy picture of the future of their city written for the Young Men's Business League in 1894.

Source: <u>New Orleans of 1894: Its Advantages, Its Prospects, Its Conditions</u>, New Orleans, 1894.

In my opinion the future of New Orleans is more promising than that of any other city upon this continent, said Mr. Fred G. Ernst, president of the Board of Trade, in the directors' room, a few mornings ago. Indeed, it has facilities for commerce that no other city possesses, situated near the sea and the natural point to which the grain and commodities of the west must come when the laws -- the natural laws of transportation -- adjust themselves. Heretofore the shipments of the west have followed the lines of immigration, going to the east. This was natural, because the railroads were first constructed from the east to develop the west and to carry away its surplus products. Then, the people of the west were for the most part allied with the people of the east by the ties of kindred and opinion. Even long after the war the poeple of Kansas and other western states had a prejudice against New Orleans. But that prejudice is a thing of the past, and the influences now at work will certainly produce their legitimate result, and New Orleans will become the market and the shipping point for an immense territory, which is constantly being developed, and which, by its commerce, will add to the material wealth of this city.

By the way, the grain convention which is to be held in New Orleans next November will be a potent factor in opening the eyes of the people of the west to the fact that New Orleans is the natural port to which their products should come. Some of our people have expressed the opinion that the new tariff law will militate against the prosperity of New Orleans. I do not believe it. Of course adjustments will have to be made under the new conditions. Some difficulties will be encountered in securing the trade of Central and South America. There are great obstacles in the way, but they are by no means insurmountable. This grain convention, or, rather, trade convention, which is to be held here in November, I honestly believe will be largely attended by delegates from the west. These men will be among the leading business men of that section, and it will be easy to make them see that their interests are ours in building up a trade with Latin America and the islands of the Pacific as soon as the Nicaragua canal is finished. As has been truly said, the balance of trade is against us to the east, and we must look to the south as a market for the products of this immense agricultural and manufacturing country. New Orleans is a natural port from which will go an immense amount of our material and food output, and the point to which will come the surplus of the Latin American counties. I do not think the tariff will cut much of a figure in the progressive march of the Crescent city. . . .

When I think of the future of New Olreans I am filled with hope, and I am firm in the belief that it is destined, like Rome, Venice and London, to become one of the great civilizing centers of the world. Here is room for a population equal to that of London and New York combined, without anybody being crowded, as is the case in those two cities. Between the river and the lake in time streets will extend, lined with handsome residences, for the commerce must ever remain in reasonable distance of the river, even with belt railroad facilities. The marshes will be drained and built upon. Difficulties to be met here are not nearly so great as the founders of Venice encountered. Nor must it be forgotten that to the east, north and west lies a vast and fertile territory, from which this city will draw its supplies and to which, in time, it must furnish the material which makes living pleasanter.

Sugar must always be a product of Louisiana soil, even with adverse legislation. It is an industry that may be crippled, but I do not believe that it can be killed. New Orleans will remain the headquarters for sugar in the United States, but though I may be accused of talking shop, I think rice is destined to become the great money crop of this state, and New Orleans will be a greater rice market than Hong Kong or any other Chinese town is to-day. Thousands upon thousands of acres that are to-day waste marsh will be converted into rice fields; thousands of people will be brought from the north and west to settle upon and cultivate these fields, all of whom will contribute to the material wealth of this city.

These are a few of the reasons for the material greatness of this city. I will only add this fact, that by its geographical position it must ever remain a railroad terminus, and in time will become one of the largest ports in the world. Of course it goes without saying that its educational, moral and artistic growth must keep pace with its increase in wealth and population.

Mr. J.C. Murphy, president of the Sugar Exchange, and one of the directors of the Young Men's Business League, in discussing the future of New Orleans said:

I am a strong believer in the future greatness of this city as a commercial and financial center. It has everything to make it forge ahead, in spite of the set-back that tariff legislation has given to sugar, one of the chief products of this state. No city in the world has a better situation for domestic and foreign commerce than New Orleans. Here is a port in which can lie at anchor the commercial navies of the world. The river upon which it is built, with its tributaries, drains a rich and populous territory, the majority of whose trade naturally belongs to New Orleans, and which will come here by the exertion of proper efforts and the furnishing of better facilities.

There is one thing of supreme importance to the future of New Orleans that is often overlooked in discussing the future of the city, that is its climate. There is no healthier city in the union, and our summers are pleasanter than those of the cities on the Atlantic seaboard. With the present quarantine arrangements there is no danger that an epidemic can be introduced into this city.

Good government is a necessity to the future of any city, and I believe that we are on the eve of securing that desirable result.

New Orleans has wonderfully improved in the past twenty years, and the proofs of progress are to be seen on every hand, but what has been done is only an earnest of what will be done in the future, for New Orleans has all the elements of a great city, and they will certainly be utilized and developed.

Mr. E.S. Stoddard, president of the Produce Exchange, has under preparation an article for a northern publication upon Louisiana, and when he was asked what his opinion was upon the future of New Orleans, replied:

This city is the entrepot of an immense territory, and without the curse of bad government would even now be one of the great cities of the world. I mean what I say, one of the great cities of the world, not of the United States only. New Olreans has a fascinating climate. It is never too cold, nor does it ever get too warm. The territory which lies about it is the richest in this land, and three months' work during the year will give to a man all the necessaries of life. You cannot say that for any other section that I know of. I am firmly persuaded that some of the difficulties that have stood in the way of progress of this city and state have been removed, and that an era of prosperity is about to set in that will be wonderful.

You know I am not to the manor born. I am from Vermont, but I have lived here for thirty years, and it is my honest opinion that there is no section with a better climate, a nobler people and whose future is brighter than that of the Crescent city.

Mr. Henry G. Hester, superintendent and secretary of the Cotton Exchange, in speaking of the future of New Orleans, remarked:

As I said to you on a future occasion this city does more business to the capital invested than any other in the United States, and I have the facts and figures to prove it. Money is turned over here faster than at any other commercial point. There is no fuss or blowing about the business done, but it is transacted.

One of the sine qua nons to the commercial prosperity of New Orleans is a clean and generous local government. A government that will aid all needed improvements, but in which no money will be squandered. That would give confidence to the capital already invested here and would induce capital to come from abroad. That is one of the difficulties that has stood in the way of the development of this city. Great strides have been made in the matter of manufacturing during the past ten years, but there is a vast field open here for improvement, especially in manufacturing. No city in the world is better situated for manufacturing plants of all kinds and no port has better facilities for transporting the output of these establishments to other markets. But bad local government has stood as a menace in the way and has blocked the road to development. . . .

THE SECOND DISTRICT INVITES TOURISTS TO ITS FRENCH MARKET
1912

> In this selection, tourists are invited by the businessmen of the second district to visit the century-old French Market "and all the live, up-to-date features of this important section." Thus history seemed to embellish the progressive spirit of these merchants.
>
> Source: <u>Some Telling Facts of the 2nd District and Famous French Market of the City of New Orleans</u>, New Orleans, 1912.

Probably no other city in America possesses a public market which is so widely known or so famed for the completeness of its arrangments for exhibiting the wares of the vendors and for the great variety of their offerings as the French Market of New Orleans. Certainly it is a most interesting place to visit, and, doubtless, there has seldom been a sightseeing visitor to New Orleans who has not roamed through its quaint arches, for the French Market is known far and wide as one of the unique features that are closely interwoven with the city's history, and one of the first objects of interest to the tourist. But once the visitor sees it he is impressed not alone with the quaintness of the buildings and the picturesquely cosmopolitan character of the market vendors and their patrons, but he realizes at a glance that here is one of the most convenient and most completely stocked markets to be found anywhere in the country, a place where one may do one's marketing with the least possible exertion, and with the reasonable certainty of finding almost anything one may want for the table. The scene presented in the market during the busy hours is one of great animation, and one who looks upon it for the first time finds himself linger with ever-increasing interest until he has seen it all in its unique phases.

Located on the river front, in the Second District, just below Jackson Square, it is one of the landmarks of New Orleans. From the very foundation of the city the site of the market was frequented by vendors of food. The Indians first bartered here, and then came the truck-gardeners from the German coast, who offered their wares here in the open air on Sunday mornings. In the year 1791 the Spaniards erected a market building, which was the first of its kind in New Orleans. This building met the requirements of the city until it was destroyed by a hurricane in 1812. Rebuilding operations were begun at once, and in the following year the existing meat market was completed on the site of the demolished building, at a cost of $30,000. The structure was of the Rusticated Doric order, which was much affected by the architects of that period. The material used was brick plastered over to imitate stone, and it had a wooden roof covered with slate. Frequent repairs to the roof have been necessary, but the remainder of the building remains practically as it was when erected. The Vegetable Market, which it was found the needs of the public demanded, was planned in 1822. It was built in two parts, one of which was completed in 1823, at a cost of $19,000, and the other in 1830, at a cost of $6,000. The entire Vegetable Market fronts 117 feet on Decatur Street. The ground plan is irregular and the style of architecture is Roman Doric. Like the Meat Market, it is built of brick, but the wooden roof, which was originally covered with tiles, is now covered with slate.

The market buildings consist mainly of wide arches supporting the roof, and it is interesting to study the old columns which support the arches along Decatur Street. Between the Meat and Vegetable Markets stands the Bazaar, which was not erected until about 1872. The Fish Market, which is a separate institution and housed in another building, just below the Fruit Market.

There is scarcely a busier place in New Orleans than the French Market from the early hours of the morning until about noon. Here the marketing of a great section of the city is done, and, indeed, so popular is this market that many persons from all over the city come here for supplies for their tables, being attracted by the great variety of meats, fish and vegetables with which this market is always stocked.

DOCUMENTS

THE BIRTH OF THE BLUES IN NEW ORLEANS BEFORE 1917

By 1917 New Orleans had become the jazz capital of the world. This selection traces the roots of this distinctive music in the black culture of the city.

Source: Frederick Ramsey, Jr. and Charles Edward Smith, Jazzmen, New York, 1939.

Early in the nineteenth century, soon after the Louisiana Purchase, slaves were allowed for the first time to assemble for social and recreational diversion. The most popular meeting place was a large open field at Orleans and Rampart, known as Congo Square. In earlier times the space had been a ceremonial ground of the Oumas Indians. Today, landscaped with palm trees, it forms a part of the municipal grounds called Beauregard Square. The Negroes, however, still speak of the place as Congo Square, in memory of the days when it was an open, dusty field, its grass worn bare by the stomping and shuffling of hundreds of restless bare feet. A century ago, slaves met there every Saturday and Sunday night to perform the tribal and sexual dances which they had brought with them from the Congo.

Before the Civil War the Congo Dances were one of the unusual sights of New Orleans to which tourists were always taken. At times almost as many white spectators as dancers gathered for the festive occasions. That the Negroes had not forgotten their dances, even after years of repression and exile from their native Africa, is attested by descriptive accounts of the times. Gaily dressed in their finest, many of the men with anklets of jingles, the Negroes rallied at the first roll of the bamboulas, large tom-toms constructed from casks covered with cowhide and beaten with two long beef bones. Galvanized by the steady, hypnotic rumble of drums, the frenzied crowd was transported to Guinea, their traditional homeland. The men, prancing, stomping and shouting, "Dansez Bamboula! Badoum! Badoum!" weaved around the women, who, swaying as their bare feet massaged the earth, intoned age-old chants. The shrieks of children around the edge of the square, as they mimicked the dancers, mingled with the cries of vendors of ginger-cakes, sweetmeats, and brilliant-hued liquors.

With the New Orleans Negro, improvisation was an essential part of musical skill, as in the case with every extra-European musician. In all cultures except that of Europe, where for a century improvisation has been a lost art, creative performance is a requisite. Thus, where there was no premium on exact repetition and hide-bound imitation, only those with the urge to express themselves and an innate power of invention took up music. When a musician could play only what he felt, those without feeling never even got started and mediocre talents soon fell by the wayside. It is important to note that the greatest talent went into dance orchestras, the only field open for those with professional musical ambitions.

The fact that these men were not primarily note readers also explains, when collective improvisation was attempted, the origin of the characteristic New Orleans polyphony, which in its more complex manifestations became a dissonant counterpoint that antedated Schoenberg.

The young New Orleans aspirant, having no teacher to show him the supposed limitations of his instrument, went ahead by himself and frequently hit upon new paths and opened up undreamed-of possibilities. In classical music the wind instruments had always lagged behind in their development. Especially the brasses were subordinated to the strings. But the freedom of the New Orleans musician from any restraining tradition and supervision enabled him to develop on most of the instruments not only new technical resources but an appropriate and unique jazz style. Incidentally, the remarkable technical equipment of many of the instrumentalists can be explained partly by the abundance of time on their hands.

So when Buddy Bolden, the barber of Franklin Street, gathered his orchestra together in the back room of his shop to try over a few new tunes for a special dance at Tin Type Hall, it was no ordinary group of musicians. Nor was Buddy an ordinary cornetist. In his day, he was entirely without competition, both in his ability as a musician and his hold upon the public. The power of his sonorous tone has never been equaled. When Buddy Bolden played in the pecan grove over in Gretna, he could be heard across the river throughout uptown New Orleans. Nor was Bolden just a musician. He was an "all-around" man. In addition to running his barber shop, he edited and published The Cricket, a scandal sheet as full of gossip as New Orleans had always been of corruption and vice. Buddy was able to scoop the field with the stories brought in by his friend, a "spider," also employed by the New Orleans police.

Carnival time always saw New Orleans in its most festive mood. It was also the busiest time for musicians. Everyone was needed in the street parades which celebrated Mardi Gras. There was at least one parade a day for the week before Mardi Gras, and on the final Tuesday, there were usually five or six. Each parade employed about fourteen bands, with a total of more than two hundred musicians. There were six gay weeks of masked balls. During the final week, balconies were decorated and maskers danced in the specially lighted streets. The parades, during the final week of pageqntry, always started at Calliope Street and St. Charles Avenue, and after going up Canal, Royal, and Orleans, ended at the site of the old Congo Square where, in the case of evening parades, the event was climaxed with a masquerade ball. . . .

THE OLD HOUSES OF THE VIEUX CARRÉ
1937

Visitors to New Orleans never forget the beauty of the old houses that line the streets of the Vieux Carré. As Stanley Clisby Arthur points out in this article, the history of the city lies embedded in the architectural development of these buildings.

Source: Stanley Clisby Arthur, Old New Orleans, A History of the Vieux Carré, Its Ancient and Historical Buildings, New Orleans, 1937.

The houses built by the original French settlers and their children were low frame structures, bricked between posts and roofed with cypress shingles. The French designated this style of architecture briquete entre poteaux, meaning literally, "bricked between posts." About 1770, during the time of the domination of Spain, the new buildings in the Vieux Carré took on increased ostentation. Many were constructed wholly of bricks and when an occasional one was built two stories high it was more magnificently classified une maison en brique et à étage (a house of brick with one story). Tile was substituted for wooden shingles; some roofs were covered with the familiar half-round red tiles, others with flat green tiles. Age-worn examples of these flat tiles from Nantes and Havre still cover a few of the old homes and are well worth observing, especially after a rain when the sun shines on their wet surfaces and brings out the verdant color baked into them. Flat tiles were used on the roofs of houses that were terraced and flower-planted after the manner of residences in Mexico City and Havana, and at sundown families repaired to these high places to enjoy what breeze might be meandering across the old town from the direction of the river.

No residence of the Old Square however grand or humble was without its courtyard or patio. Houses being built as they were flush with the banquette, as the sidewalk was called, to gain entrance to the court one passed through the porte cochère, a wide gate usually constructed of thick planks then through a high-domed passageway that tunneled the ground floor structure. This corridor was sufficiently wide to admit a brace of horses drawing the family carriage called a calèche découverte. The opening to the patio was high enough to prevent the negro coachman with his towering beaver hat from being knocked from his perch on the carriage seat.

To the French the flagged or bricked "backyard" was a cour, but with the coming of the Spanish the term patio was used and remained in favor. There was usually a fountain in the center of the patio and a well-planned garden or <u>parterre,</u> or at least a collection of potted plants to enliven the walled-in court with green leaves and bright flowers. Huge wide-mouthed and pot-bellied earthen jars that had carried overseas the oil from the olive groves of Spain found their way into the garden and were used to catch the rain water from the roof gutters and down-spouts, and today the old jars or <u>ollas</u> are considered distincly decorative features of any Old Square courtyard. Occupying one or two sides of the court were the kitchen and slave quarters, buildings always detached from the main dwelling, and in the rear were the carriage house and stalls for the horses.

The broad stairs which led to the living apartments of the main house were built in the patio under the shelter of a "gallery" or upstairs porch, but more usually they led upstairs from the corridor. Houses of true Spanish construction can be recognized at a glance by the window openings which are wide, arched at the top, and frequently without a prominent keystone. Over many, and especially above entrances indoors and out, are to be seen the celebrated fan transoms, distinctive features in these architectural relics of Old New Orleans' <u>Vieux Carré</u>. Sills of the windows that opened on the courtyards were made generously wide to hold flower pots, for the Creoles were then as now fond of growing things, and few homes were without little pots of fragrant rosemary. Aside from its medicinal properties rosemary was the "flower for remembrance" and was believed to keep an absent lover's thoughts continually on the fair one left behind. Consequently, these plants were diligently tended.

Two disastrous fires visited New Orleans during the Spanish regime, the first in 1788, the second in 1794. One of the orders issued by Governor the Baron de Carondelet after the second conflagration ordained that all homes in the center of the city, built more than one story high, be reconstructed of brick, and Spanish police regulations also decreed the kind of timber to be used--cypress which must be felled at certain periods of the year, and, incredible but true, only during certain <u>phases of the moon</u>! It was believed that the wood thus secured would be well seasoned and free from decay. Today, notwithstanding the inroads of time and the ravages of age and a damp, sub-tropical climate, many of the buildings in the heart of the <u>Vieux Carré</u> remain remarkably preserved specimens of the splendid architecture of the Spanish Creoles.

The bricks used in the construction of these buildings were made from a peculiar sandy clay found along the banks of the Mississippi and even within the embrace of the famed crescent bend. When removed from the kilns, the bricks had a peculiar texture -- they could be rubbed together and reduced, without much effort, to a mass of yellowish-red powder. Yet they served their purpose admirably when employed in erecting high buildings. To make one brick adhere to another, a native cement or mortar was used. It is claimed that the secret of this cement has been lost, like that of the old Roman cement used in building the <u>Via Appia,</u> but chemists of today know why this cement of the builders of 1795 compares in hardness and durability with materials now in use. This mortar of old New Orleans was made from lime secured by burning clam shells still abundant in nearby Lake Ponchartrain and other lake bottoms. When unsaturated with moisture, this mortar becomes a binder even of harder substance than the bricks it holds so firmly together. However, to keep the soft bricks from eroding and the mortar from becoming wet, it was found necessary to plaster the exterior of the structure. That is why the old buildings of the French Quarter are always covered with plaster, and why, when the plaster has fallen away in patches on some ancient structure, the exposed bricks are worn and rounded from the rain and the mortar has crumbled from between them.

REFORMING THE POLICE DEPARTMENT
1946

World War II deeply altered the social structure of American cities and created new problems for those responsible for the maintenance of law and order. In an attempt to reform the New Orleans police department, this survey was prepared by the city government. This selection reveals not only the concern for the shifting population of the city but also the attitudes and goals of the city planners of this period.

Source: Bruce Smith, <u>New Orleans Police Survey</u>, New Orleans, 1946.

THE NEW ORLEANS POLICE SURVEY

  The community setting of the police department offers some unusual features. New Orleans has a blend of national strains and cultures that is absolutely unique among the larger American cities, and a larger proportion of Negro inhabitants than any city over 350,000 population. Such extremes can profoundly influence both the aims and the functioning of law enforcement. Since New Orleans is both a river town, with all of its implications, and a great seaport that faces Latin America, an uncounted floating population also complicates certain of the police problems that arise out of crime and disorder.
  From some or all of the foregoing factors is derived the city's widely heralded and locally accepted reputation as a community not suffering from puritanical inhibitions. While this is a matter that is exclusively the city's own affair, it is pertinent to state that whatever the policies with respect to prostitution, liquor and gambling, they must be clearly defined, openly declared and consistently applied. Complete toleration until certain undisclosed bounds are exceeded always results in uneven enforcement and deprives the police administrator of any standard to which he can hold his subordinates. Formal or informal "protection," with attendant graft and widening circles of corruption are certain to follow, while exposure, civic wrath and political overturns succeed in dreary cycle and often settle nothing.
  Despite these features serving to set New Orleans apart from the general American scene, its police service differs chiefly in the lag that has characterized the adoption of tried and tested methods. It is still deficient in its use of modern means of transport and communication, while in selecting, training, promoting and disciplining the rank and file, in distributing the available manpower, and in producing unity of action from the many

parts of a necessarily complex organism, the force stands only at the threshold of an extensive area long since occupied by more enterprising police agencies.

The administrative structure of the police department is also unusually loose, and in some respects is ill-fitted for the task in hand. Essential interrelationships among the many independent units in the department either are vaguely defined or do not exist. Over-specialization of function characterizes some of these units to an extraordinary degree, while the continuous flow of certain processes is blocked and impeded by defective organization and intra-force rivalries that flourish unchecked by an effective discipline.

Police of all ranks have been originally selected and later advanced in authority and in compensation, without recourse to recognized personnel procedures. Although the police force was brought under the jurisdiction of the city civil service commission in 1943, the unsettling effects of the war period made it either impossible or inadvisable to introduce the new personnel procedures and control on any extensive scale.

In these and other respects the force is now in a transitional stage, with many changes proposed or impending, but with the issue in doubt. Such widespread uncertainties are quickly imparted to the rank and file, and throughout the department one accordingly finds much anxiety for what the immediate future may hold, an accelerated tendency towards relaxed discipline, and many individual efforts towards self-aggrandizement in what is expected to be a general shakeup.

Such disturbing features are in part unavoidable at such a time, but they are also the direct product of inferior organization and administration. The uneasy atmosphere now pervading police headquarters and precinct stations would be far less pronounced, and would have less effect upon the day-to-day performance of police duty, if just and exacting disciplinary controls had ever been applied in any considerable degree. But these moderating influences have been so conspicuously lacking that the confidence of police in the effectiveness of the complex organism of which they are a part, and even their trust in each other, has been seriously impaired. The go-as-you-please race carried on for decades has now turned into stampede and headlong rout.

The underlying conditions here described appear not to be the marks left by any one period in the police department's history; on the contrary the clear indications are that they have prevailed for a long time, and probably trace their origins back to the earliest days of police service in this city. Hence it will be unproductive to apply the main effort at extensive changes among the directing heads. The fault and the responsibility lie much deeper than that, and can be corrected only by thorough-going change in administrative organization and practices.

The police force seemingly has never been well or effectively organized, has never been adequately supervised and controlled by higher authority, has never experienced any large degree of independence from partisan influence, and hence has never developed any morale of its own which would serve to keep it functioning before, during and after changes of political control. Its continuing state of instability prevents the development of improved administrative practices long since adopted in most other large American cities together with some hundreds of communities of moderate size. The seeds of the great advances made by police service generally during the past two or three decades have not found favorable soil here, and though some have feebly sprouted, they fail to take firm root and wither in the first political blast to strike them.

It is no light talks to reverse a course established for generations, to excise personal and structural decay, and to raise a new and more imposing structure upon secure foundations. Yet nothing less than a fresh start, according to new plans, and with firm resolves persistently adhered to, can hope to offset the neglect of these many years. It follows that any program holding hope for success must be applied over a lengthy period, and that confidence in both the means employed and in the ultimate objective must carry far beyond temporary enthusiasms. It is the purpose of this survey to lay down the outlines of such means and such ends, and particularly to indicate those critical points to which special attention must be given if a favorable result is to be secured. The plans themselves will mean little or nothing unless they commend themselves to constituted authority, are actually adopted, and vigorously pursued. While every effort has been made to adapt them to the special conditions here prevailing, they all rest upon successful police practices in many communities, and if applied without destructive compromise they will produce good and perhaps superior results here.

CITY PLANNING FOR METROPOLITAN NEW ORLEANS
1948

By the late 1940s the relationship between inner-city New Orleans and its metropolitan area became critical. This report and the selections from it which follow was prepared by a firm of professional city planners and submitted to the City Planning and Zoning Commission in November, 1946.

Source: <u>Report of Harland Bartholomew and Associates to the New Orleans City Planning and Zoning Commission</u>, New Orleans, 1948.

LOCAL TRENDS PRIOR TO 1940

Between 1810 and 1840 New Orleans grew very rapidly, having a considerably larger rate of increase than urban United States. During this period New Orleans was substantially the only urban community in Louisiana, and the population curves for New Orleans and urban Louisiana are almost coincident for those years. Between 1840 and 1890 population growth in New Orleans was not as rapid as in the state, nor as rapid as in the United States as a whole. During this period population growth in New Orleans was almost constant, at a rate of about 13% per decade as compared with national and state rates of about 30% per decade.

From 1890 to 1930 New Orleans again had an unusually constant rate of growth, but the rate increased to about 18% per decade. During this period the rates of growth for Louisiana and the United States as a whole averaged about the same as for New Orleans but the rates of growth for Louisiana and for the United States were decreasing while the rate of growth of New Orleans remained nearly constant. However, several other cities in Louisiana experienced more rapid rates of increase than did New Orleans. Population growth figures for New Orleans and metropolitan New Orleans in relation to the population of Louisiana, urban Louisiana, the United States and urban United States are given in Table A of the Appendix.

Prior to 1890 almost all of the population of metropolitan New Orleans had been within the City, but between 1890 and 1930 that part of the metropolitan area beyond the corporate limits of the City began to experience a steady increase in population growth. A New Orleans metropolitan district was established by the United States Census in 1910 but the area embraced within this metropolitan district was smaller than the area included for the years 1930 and 1940. . . .

The figure given for the 1920 population of the metropolitan district is an estimate prepared by the Southern Bell Telephone Company for the area embraced within the present metropolitan census district, based on United States Census enumeration district figures. The population of that part of the metropolitan area which is beyond the corporate limits of New Orleans increased from approximately 26,000 in 1920 to 36,115 in 1930. This represents an increas of 38% as compared with an increase of 18.5% within the city.

Between 1930 and 1940 population within the city of New Orleans increased only 7.8%, approximately the same as the urban population of the United States. However, the population of the state increased more and the population of other cities in Louisiana increased much more than that of New Orleans. During this decade the death rate in New Orleans decreased while that for the United States remained the same, and the birth rate for New Orleans increased while that for the United States decreased. This increase in the birth rate and decrease in the death rate in a decade of comparatively little population increase indicates that between 1930 and 1940 large numbers of people did not migrate into New Orleans from outside areas.

LOCAL TRENDS SINCE 1940

The 1945 estimates for New Orleans and metropolitan New Orleans were prepared by the New Orleans Committee for Economic Development under the supervision of the Bureau of Business Research of Louisiana State University. These estimates are based on a 5% sample survey and did not cover the entire area embraced within the New Orleans metropolitan district as defined by the United States Census. However, all available information indicates that the 1945 estimate for metropolitan New Orleans would be increased by not more than 1% if it were expanded to include all of the area embraced by the metropolitan census district.

These 1945 estimates compared favorably with unofficial estimates based on data compiled by local private corporations and with data obtained from building permits issued in the City of New Orleans. In addition, a recent estimate for metropolitan New Orleans by the United States Bureau of the Census checks very closely with the Committee for Economic Development estimate of 1945. . . .

The Committee for Economic Development estimate reveals that the population of New Orleans in 1945 was 548,120. and the population of metropolitan New Orleans was approximately 601,800. This gives a population increase of 10.8% over 1940 in the City and an increase of 11.4% in the entire metropolitan district. This is almost twice as large an increase as is indicated for the state and for the United States as a whole for this five-year period. It also represents a population increase in New Orleans and believed to be reasonable, these estimates have been used as one of the bases for determining the probable future population of New Orleans and its metropolitan area. . . .

THE "HOME RULE" CHARTER OF NEW ORLEANS, 1954

On May 1, 1954 the city adopted its ninth charter since 1805. This charter, which has remained in effect until the present, established a mayor-council form of government. The extracts from this charter reveal some of the characteristics of the present home rule municipal government of New Orleans.

Source: <u>Home Rule Charter of the City of New Orleans</u>, New Orleans, 1954.

PREAMBLE

We, the people of the City of New Orleans and Parish of Orleans, trusting in God and grateful to Him for the freedoms we enjoy, do ordain, establish, approve, and adopt this Home Rule Charter pursuant to Section 22 of Article XIV of the Constitution of the State of Louisiana, as amended by Act 551 of 1950. . . .

Section 1-101. Incorporation. The inhabitants of the City of New Orleans, within the boundaries now established by law or as may hereafter be established, shall be and continue a body politic and corporate by the name of "City of New Orleans," hereinafter in this Charter called "City." By that name it shall have perpetual succession and enjoy all of the powers hereinafter recited.

Section 1-102. Form of Government. The government provided by this Charter shall be known as the Mayor-Council form of government. The Mayor shall be aided by a Chief Administrative Officer who, in the performance of his duties, shall be responsible to the Mayor. . . .

Section 2-101. Powers. (1) The City shall retain, to the same extent as if herein repeated, all rights, powers, privileges and authority that it has or could claim under the law of this State at the time of the adoption hereof, except as herein expressly modified.

(2) In addition to the foregoing, the City shall have all rights, powers, privileges and authority herein conferred or herein enlarged, and all rights, powers, privileges and authority whether expressed or implied that may hereafter be granted to a similar corporation by any general law of the State, or that may be necessary or useful to enjoy a home rule charter.

(3) The rights, powers, privileges and authority heretofore enjoyed, herein retained or herein claimed shall subsist, notwithstanding the repeal of any law, until any such right, power, privilege or authority be altered or taken away by amendment to this Charter in the manner provided for by the Constitution.

(4) The City, in addition to the rights, powers, privileges and authority expressly conferred upon it by this Charter, shall have the right, power, privilege and authority to adopt and enforce local police, sanitary and similar regulations, and to do and perform all of the acts

pertaining to its local affairs, property and government, which are necessary or proper in the legitimate exercise of its corporate powers and municipal functions.

(5) No enumeration of any rights, power, privilege or authority hereinafter made, and no repeal of any law under which the City derives any right, power, privilege or authority, shall be construed as limiting or abolishing any right, power, privilege or authority hereinabove set forth. . . .

Section 3-101. Legislative Powers. (1) All legislative powers of the City shall be vested in the Council and exercised by it in the manner and subject to the limitations hereinafter set forth.

(2) The Council shall have the right to levy any and all classes of taxes, excises, licenses and fees necessary for the proper operation and maintenance of the municipality for the payment of debt, and for capital improvements that are not expressly prohibited by the Constitution.

Section 3-102. Number and Terms of Councilmen. The Council shall consist of seven members, of whom five shall be elected from districts and two from the City at large. The terms of councilmen shall be four years beginning on the first Monday in May next following their election except that a councilman selected to fill a vacancy shall serve only for the remainder of the unexpired term.

Section 3-103. Councilmanic Districts. (1) The City shall be divided into five Councilmanic Districts. Each District shall serve as the basis for electing a district councilman. The five Districts shall be as follows:

(a) District "A" shall be composed of the Fourteenth Ward, the Fifteenth Ward, the Sixteenth Ward, and the Seventeenth Ward.

(b) District "B" shall be composed of the First Ward, the Tenth Ward, the Eleventh Ward, the Twelfth Ward, and the Thirteenth Ward.

(c) District "C" shall be composed of the Second Ward, the Third Ward, the Fourth Ward, the Fifth Ward, and the Sixth Ward.

(d) District "D" shall be composed of the Seventh Ward, and the Eighth Ward.

(e) District "E" shall be composed of the Ninth Ward.

(2) The wards referred to in this Section shall mean the seventeen wards of the City existing at the effective date of this Charter.

(3) It shall be the mandatory duty of the Council to redistrict the City by ordinance within six months after the official publication by the United States of the population of the City as enumerated in each decennial census. Each councilmanic district shall contain as nearly as possible the population factor obtained by dividing by five the City's population as shown by the decennial census. At the expiration of the six months period, if the Council shall have failed to redistrict the City as herein required, the members of the Council shall not receive any further salaries until the Council shall have adopted such ordinance, which may not be vetoed by the Mayor, and the Director of Finance shall not issue

checks for such salaries for said periods.

Section 3-104. Qualifications of Councilmen. A councilman shall be a citizen of the United States and a qualified elector of the City, and shall not hold any other public office or position, the office of Notary Public, and office in the military or naval forces excepted. Candidates for Councilmen-at-large shall have been residents of the City for two years immediately preceding their election. Candidates for district councilmen shall have been residents of the districts from which elected for at least two years immediately preceding their election. Any councilman who removes his residence from the City or from the district from which he was elected shall thereby vacate his office.

THE NEW ORLEANS SCHOOL CRISIS OF 1960

On July 16, 1959, Federal Judge J. Skelly Wright raised the curtain on a drama involving the desegregation of the New Orleans school system. The next year, on November 16, a racial explosion occurred that has come to be known as the "School Crisis of 1960." This crisis and its embattled forces are admirably analyzed in the selections that follow.

Source: The New Orleans School Crisis: Report of the Louisiana State Advisory Committee to the United States Commission on Civil Rights, Washington, D.C., 1961.

The school crisis in New Orleans was one of the most significant events of 1960, not only for the United States but for the entire world. Race relations is the most momentous domestic problem in our country. With the rising nationalism and ethnocentrism of the emerging countries of Africa and Asia, the problem of race relations (aside from war and peace) is probably the most consequential social issue facing the planet.

Strains and stresses in white-Negro relations in the United States have come to a sharp focus in the conflict over desegregating the Nation's public schools. The conflict is not restricted to the South, but it is there that the polarization of opposing forces is most acute and most intense. In the fall of 1960, the conflict assumed explosive proportions in New Orleans. Fortunately, the majority of citizens--of Southern citizens too-- are law-abiding, and the explosion was limited.

Yet, the conflict smoulders and the final solution is not clear. We hope that wise and cool minds will prevail over the "Hotspurs" of Louisiana, for the whole world now looks to us, judging our conduct as it affects history and world relations.

In the interest of preserving and strengthening the civil rights of all our countrymen, white or Negro, we would like to tell the story of the New Orleans school crisis, as we see it. To those who object to our views, please remember the words of Alfred North Whitehead: "If it is an uninterpreted fact that you seek, go ask a stone to tell you its autobiography."

It is a long established fact that leadership takes on added significance during periods of social crises. Therefore, it should be instructive to analyze the role of leadership during the 1960-61 school desegregation crisis in New Orleans.

As in any other metropolis, leadership in New Orleans is diverse. The "leadership class" is composed of every significant element of the city's population. Since the interests and goals of the several social segments differ in some important particulars, the attitudes, opinions, and activities of the leaders, though overlapping on certain important issues, will tend toward diversity, even conflict, on certain other major issues.

No other issue in recent history has affected New Orleans so widely and deeply as has the issue of racial desegregation in public education. So fundamental is this issue that it touches directly or indirectly every aspect of community life. This section of the report describes the way the "leadership class" responded (or failed to respond) to the school crisis.

Immediately following the May 1954 United States Supreme Court decision, a new organization was founded in New Orleans. It is called the White Citizens Council. This organization is composed of a relatively few, but extremely rabid white supremacists. The expressed purpose of this organization is to preserve "total segregation." This organization, of course, focused its attention primarily upon the preservation of segregation in public education, though from time to time it emphasizes the importance of maintaining segregation in other areas of community life.

Since education involves children, and since children represent the hopes, the aspirations, as well as the fears and failures of parents, it was not long before the question of desegregation of the public schools in New Orleans became an explosive issue. The segregationists resurrected every fearful and despicable Negro stereotype in their efforts to influence the minds of white parents.

Using every medium at their disposal, they pictured Negroes as lazy and shiftless, mentally inferior, dirty, immoral, criminal, diseased, violent, savage, "pushy and uppity," conspicuous and boisterous in their behavior, and under the influence of communist-inspired leaders.

These stereotypes, and more, were eloquently expounded by the most rabid segregationists in the State and many influential segregationists from out of the State. In fact, a list of the segregationists who appeared at mass meetings of the White Citizens Council of New Orleans would read like a "who's who among white supremacists." Among the speakers were influential public figures from many other Southern States. Also appearing at these mass meetings at one time or another were the "top" white supremacists of Louisiana including: Judge Leander Perez; Governor Jimmy H. Davis; State Senator William Rainach; Emile Wagner (school board member); Attorney General Jack P.F. Gremillion; State Superintendent of Education Shelby M. Jackson; and Dr. Emmett L. Irwin (president, White Citizens Council of New Orleans).

In addition to the "top" segregationist leaders whose names are listed above, the White Citizens Council in New Orleans frequently presented "lesser lights" who spoke to smaller groups. Furthermore, many public figures, such as outstanding business and professional men, and national and State political figures--particularly candidates for public office--were pressed into making strong statements about segregation. Also, they were maneuvered into encouraging "civil disobedience," since they deny the validity of the Brown decision, as well as the possibility of its enforcement. It was not surprising that the White Citizens Council became politically powerful in a very short time.

The values, traditions, and fears propagandized by this segregationist organization are essentially rural. Consequently, since the Louisiana State legislature is dominated by representatives of rural communities, it began immediately to pass a rash of anti-Negro laws designed to preserve what the lawmakers termed "Southern traditions." Some of these "Black Codes" were obviously unconstitutional, even to the lawmakers themselves. They were passed for the avowed purpose of circumventing Federal court decision, or at least, as delaying tactics.

Unfortunately the rural conservatism of State politics had a profound effect on the situation in New Orleans as a mayor with a liberal reputation found it necessary to moderate his position in his drive for the governorship. This change of position came as a shock to the mayor's perennial supporters and dealt a crushing blow to the hopes of Orleanians that the office of mayor would prove a source of strength and leadership for open schools. The White Citizens Council took advantage of this absence of official leadership, and by default became the dominant political force in the community in the education crisis. Mayor Morrison must accept much of the responsibility for the atmosphere thus created.

The main targets of the White Citizens Council were the NAACP, which was labeled as communist-dominated; the United States Supreme Court, which was accused of usurping legislative prerogatives and substituting sociological theory for legal precedents; and white liberals, whom the council subtly accused of being either communists or dupes of communist conspirators. This propaganda is apparently without foundation, because, during the long months of bitter controversy, no concrete evidence to substantiate these accusations has been produced.

Joining in support of the program of the White Citizens Council were numerous neighborhood organizations, which met regularly in order to give lesser white supremacists an opportunity to express themselves on the issue of public school desegregation. Some of these leaders base their contentions on far-fetched rationales. An example of this is a statement by Mrs. B.J. Gaillat, Jr., president of Save Our Nation, Inc., in which she contends that there is ample evidence that the Bible and the Catholic Church both support racial segregation. She declared, "The issue is not one of hate, violence, or disobedience. Rather it is one of obedience to God's law. God gave Moses the Law of Segregation on Mount Sinai. . . ."

Throughout all this crisis, the most abused leader in New Orleans was Federal Judge J. Skelly Wright. Time after time, it was his difficult duty to set aside State laws, overrule the State administration orders, and place practically every public official under restraining orders to prevent interference with the desegregation of McDonogh No. 19 and William Frantz Elementary Schools.

The January 30th banquet which some private white citizens held in honor of the four "moderate" members of the school board and Superintendent James Redmond, who kept the schools open in spite of all manner of legal, extra-legal, and illegal harassment, may have been the turning point in the desegregation crisis. More than 1,600 citizens attended this banquet. The guests of honor were given hearty and sincere acclaim. Insofar as the issue of public school desegregation is concerned, by far the largest segment of leaders in New Orleans may be classified as "neutrals." Included in this category are influential leaders in business, labor relations, politics, the professions, and civic and social affairs.

During the long and bitter controversy over the moral, legal, and social aspects of desegregation, the vast majority of the "top" leadership in New Orleans made no public statement in regard to this all-important issue. The truth is that, time and time again, they refused to speak out, despite the fact that certain other responsible citizens begged them to do so. It was not until the school crisis had already developed to a critical point that a "hundred" of these leaders began to issue cautious statements intended to create a favorable climate for the preservation of public education in spite of "token" desegregation. Generally, the statements issued by them were designed to discourage lawlessness. . . .

The contest between State and Federal authorities over whether or not public schools in Louisiana will remain segregated, become desegragated, or close altogether has been so tense that only a few white leaders, mostly in religion, have dared to identify themselves as desegregationists. Thus, during the several weeks of the most intense crisis, some white religious leaders and a few religious organizations made public pronouncements to the effect that racial segregation is morally wrong and that the United States Supreme Court was legally correct in outlawing it in public education. A handful of white civic leaders made similar statements, but no important white organization so declared itself. . . .

Therefore, by and large, the active desegregationists in New Orleans are Negroes.

It is a widely known fact that Negro leaders are likely to be divided on many social issues. Nevertheless, where the desegregation of public education is concerned, they present a united front. All segments of leadership in the Negro community have publicly expressed a strong desire to see racial segregation in public education abolished immediately.

The only noticeable difference of opinion among Negro leaders regarding the desegregation issue concerns the degree of difficulty involved in bringing about compliance with Federal court rulings.

Some are optimistic. They visualize an end of segregation in public education in New Orleans almost immediately. They predict that the boycott in effect at the two desegregated schools will be substantially broken by September 1961 and that a considerably larger number of Negro children will be admitted to desegregated classes.

Other Negro leaders constantly warn their followers to brace themselves for years of costly litigation and bitter racial feelings before desegregation becomes a reality.

Perhaps the most interesting strategy Negro leaders have employed during this desegregation crisis is this: most of the "top" Negro leadership have advocated that Negroes play a "waiting game"--sit back and allow this issue to be legally decided in the courts and implemented by white "moderates."

Prior to the crisis (between 1952-58), the NAACP did have occasional mass meetings, at which time reports were made in regard to the Bush v. New Orleans Board of Education case. At these meetings, money was raised to support the NAACP. However, there have been no public demonstrations, no lawlessness, no attempts to threaten or intimidate those who opposed the association, and few attempts to publicize the case for desegregation. By and large, Negro leaders have defined this as a legal, constitutional fight which they feel confident will be won by sane, stable local and national leaders.

Perhaps the most serious blunder made by white leaders in New Orleans is that they have failed to utilize the knowledge, wisdom, and insight of established Negro leaders in their attempt to achieve some orderly pattern in the public education controversy. At no time have the city or State officials sought the advice or counsel of informed Negro leaders, despite the fact that on numerous occasions Negro leaders have volunteered their services.

Certain city officials have said that the violence, disorder, and racial hatred that New Orleans experienced during recent months was caused largely by "outsiders" and a few uninformed, irresponsible local whites. They may, in some measure, be right. It seems certain, however, that the ugly mobs would not have formed if they had not felt certain of the approval or at least the indifference of influential white leaders, some of whom appeared to use the crisis for political ends. . . .

PLAN TO PRESERVE THE VIEUX CARRÉ, 1968

Expansion of American cities has often been achieved at the expense of its historical monuments and districts. Stimulated as much by tourism as by aesthetics, the move to preserve the Vieux Carré began in the 1920s. The Plan of 1968 was part of a historic district demonstration study and represents the culmination of many efforts to assure the preservation of this beautiful part of the city.

Source: <u>Plan</u> <u>and</u> <u>Program</u> <u>for</u> <u>the</u> <u>Preservation</u> <u>of</u> <u>the</u> <u>Vieux</u> <u>Carré</u>, New Orleans, 1968.

Goals and Policies

This part of the report presents the recommended Plan for the Vieux Carré and a program of action to implement the proposals contained in the Plan. The Plan consists of interrelated long-range, intermediate, and short-range components, so that proposals for more immediate action can be understood within the framework of long-range goals for the preservation of the historic district.

Proposed Long-Range Goals

The long-range goals for the Vieux Carré can be stated as follows:

1. Preserve the Vieux Carré as a historic district of national significance.
2. Guide change to insure the historical continuity of the Vieux Carré's environmental unity, its tout ensemble.
3. Improve the quality of the Vieux Carré's environment by eliminating incompatible and undesirable uses and structures, providing needed amenities and services, and strengthening incentives and controls to improve design standards for new construction and for the rehabilitation of existing buildings.
4. Realize the Vieux Carré's physical, social, and economic potential as an important tourist center, a resource for the people of the metropolitan area, a desirable in-town residential district, a focal area for the arts and crafts, a major shopping and entertainment complex, and a vital part of the city's economic and tax base.
5. Provide needed facilities and services to support and enhance the functioning of the historic district for serving visitors, residents, and workers.
6. Provide facilities to improve traffic circulation, transit service, and automobile storage within the historic district consistent with proper environmental standards.

Proposed Policies

To achieve these long-range goals for the Vieux Carré, a statement of policies is needed to guide everyday decisions by a variety of public agencies concerned with the preservation and improvement of the historic district. Agreement on basic policies can serve to coordinate these daily decisions in terms of long-range goals and assist private individuals in making better investment decisions.

Preservation Policies

1. Preservation should encompass both the physical and functional elements of the Vieux Carré that contribute to its identity and environmental unity.
2. Public action should be especially directed at retaining and strengthening the Quarter's diversity and authenticity.
3. The Vieux Carré should be continued as a living, functioning community, not a museum complex.
4. The quality of rehabilitation-restoration work in the Vieux Carré should be improved through positive programs of financial and technical assistance as well as the application of such negative controls as zoning and building regulations.
5. The maintenance and repair of buildings of architectural and historic significance should be assured by public action where necessary.
6. Individual structures should be continued in uses that are compatible with their architectural character.
7. Changes in density resulting from rehabilitation should be carefully controlled.
8. Systematic code enforcement should be carried out within the Quarter to upgrade existing building conditions and prevent demolition by neglect.

Development Policies

1. Development should be channelled to remove obsolete buildings and renew declining sub-areas within the Quarter, and should be diverted away from the historic core where older structures are concentrated.
2. New buildings should be carefully related to existing structures in terms of height, material, color, form, and site plan and should honestly express present-day requirements.
3. New construction should be consistent in design and location with the existing historic context and architectural setting.
4. Physical development should be planned to delineate more strongly the physical limits of the Vieux Carré with the Mississippi reestablished as the natural physical boundary of the Quarter.
5. The pattern of development within the Vieux Carré and centers of activity adjoining the Quarter, especially the International Trade Mart, the central retail area, and the proposed new

cultural center should be closely related to one another.
6. The range of available facilities within the Vieux Carré should be greatly expanded, including additional facilities for tourists and visitors, community facilities for local residents, and supporting cultural and entertainment activities for out-of-town visitors and city and Vieux Carré residents.
7. A system of public and private open space should be developed to provide an internal physical structure to the Quarter and reestablish the visual and physical link between the riverfront and the area of original settlement.
8. Historic open spaces and similar features should be recreated wherever feasible to serve modern needs for amenity and use.

Transportation Policies

1. The requirements of the automobile should be recognized but subordinated to the need for preserving the quality of the historic environment.
2. Internal circulation, service, and goods-handling within the Quarter should be improved with through traffic diverted from local streets.
3. Conflicts between pedestrian and vehicular traffic should be minimized and the quality of the pedestrian environment greatly upgraded.
4. An internal transit system for tourists and others should be established.
5. The Riverfront Expressway should be carefully designed to reduce its negative impact on the Quarter.
6. Parking facilities should be expanded to provide for future demands and properly located to minimize future disruption.

BIBLIOGRAPHY

This annotated bibliography contains the keys to countless aspects of the incredibly rich history of the city of New Orleans. The books and articles included were carefully chosen on the basis of their scholarly character and usefulness for further research. Thus, the bibliographies in these specialized books greatly expand the student's contact with the best that has been written on any subject.

An indispensible source for the serious student of the city is the journal Louisiana History that before 1960 was called The Louisiana Historical Quarterly. A selection of articles from this source has been included in this bibliography. Also, the newspaper The Daily Picayune has chronicled events in the city for more than a century, it is a first-rate primary source and can be found on microfilm in larger libraries.

The manuscript sources for the history of New Orleans are dispersed throughout the United States and Europe. For the French colonial period one should consult the Archives Nationales at Paris, France. The Archivo General de Indias in Seville, Spain, and the Spanish Judicial Records in the Louisiana State Museum contain important material on the Spanish period. See also the Manuscripts Division of the Library of Congress Library, Washington, D.C.; the Reports of the Board of Police Commissioners, Records of the Deliberations of the Cabildo (1769-1803); Mayors' Messages to Municipality No. 1 (1804-1853), and The City Council Minutes and Resolutions, all in New Orleans. The New Orleans Public Library at 219 Loyola Avenue contains important materials on all phases of the city and its history.

BIBLIOGRAPHY

Adams, William H. "New Orleans as the National Center of Boxing," Louisiana Historical Quarterly, vol. XXXIX, no. 1 (1956).

Alwes, Berchtold C. "The History of the Louisiana State Lottery," Louisiana Historical Quarterly, vol. 27, no. 4 (October, 1944).

Asbury, Herbert. The French Quarter: An Informal History of the New Orleans Underworld, New York: 1936. Panorama of New Orleans; thorough job in "washing the dirty linen" of the city; highly entertaining rather than scholarly, but contains a bibliography.

Basso, Etolia Simmons, (ed.) The World from Jackson Square: A New Orleans Reader; with introduction by Hamilton Basso, New York: 1948. A remarkable collection of readings by some of the best writers who have written about New Orleans.

Baudier, Roger. The Catholic Church in Louisiana, New Orleans: 1939.

Berr, William. "Louisiana History on Government Documents," The Gulf States Historical Magazine, vol. 1 (November, 1921).

Biever, Albert Hubert, S. J. The Jesuits in New Orleans and the Mississippi Valley, New Orleans: 1924.

Blain, Hugh Mercer. A Near Century of Public Service in New Orleans: The Story of the Origins and Progress of the Gas, Street Railways and Electric Service in New Orleans, New Orleans: 1927.

Blassingame, John W. Black New Orleans, 1860-1880, Chicago: 1973. A social history, based on a vast variety of primary sources.

Bolding, Gary A. "The New Orleans Seaway Movement," Louisiana History, vol. X (1969).

Boyle, James Ernest. Cotton and the New Orleans Cotton Exchange, Garden City, New York: 1934.

Brooks, Charles B. The Siege of New Orleans, Seattle: 1961. Well researched, with maps and detailed descriptions of the military engagements on both sides.

Burson, Caroline M. The Stewardship of Don Estaban Miro: 1782-1792, New Orleans: 1940.

Butler, Benjamin F. The Autobiography and Personal Reminiscenses of Major-General Benjamin F. Butler, Boston: 1892.

Cable, George W. The Creoles of Louisiana, With Introduction and Note by Arlin Turner, New York: 1970. An excellent new edition of a classic written in 1874.

Caldwell, Stephen A. A Banking History of Louisiana, Baton Rouge: 1935.

Capers, Gerald M. Occupied City -- New Orleans Under the Federals, 1862-1865, Lexington: 1965.

Carrigan, Jo Ann. "Yellow Fever in New Orleans, 1853: Abstractions and Realities," Journal of Southern History. (August, 1959).

Carter, Hodding, (ed.) The Past as Prelude: New Orleans 1718-1968, New Orleans: 1968. A collection of important essays.

Chenault, William W. and Robert C. Reinders. "The Northern-Born Community of New Orleans in the 1850's," Journal of American History, vol. II (September, 1964).

Chidsey, Donald Barr. Battle of New Orleans: An Informal History of the War that Nobody Wanted, New York: 1962. Written with style; it contains an extensive bibliography and some documents.

_____. Louisiana Purchase, New York: 1972. Contains a good bibliography.

Clark, John G. "New Orleans: Its First Century of Economic Development," Louisiana History, vol. X (1969).

_____. New Orleans, An Economic History: 1718-1812, Baton Rouge: 1970. The first comprehensive interpretation of the economic history of the colonial period; well written.

Clisby, Arthur S. Old New Orleans: A History of the Vieux Carré. New Orleans: 1937.

Coulter, Ellis Morton, (ed.) The Other Half of Old New Orleans, Baton Rouge: 1939. Interesting sketches published by the New Orleans Picayune during the years 1840 to 1842, probably authored by George W. Kendall (an editor of the Picayune).

Coxe, John E. "The New Orleans Mafia Incident," Louisiana Historical Quarterly, vol. 20, no. 4 (1937).

Cross, Robert Allen. A History of Southern Methodism in New Orleans, New Orleans: 1931.

Curtis, Nathaniel. Orleans: Its Old Houses, Shops, and Public Buildings, Philadelphia: 1933. Uses simple, non-technical language to describe the architectural lore of the city.

Dabney, Thomas Ewing. One Hundred Years: The Story of the Times Picayune from its Founding to 1940, Baton Rouge: 1944.

Davis, Edwin Adams. Louisiana: A Narrative History, Baton Rouge: 1965. A useful work of reference prepared with care.

Duffy, John. The Rudolph Matas History of Medicine in Louisiana, 2 vols., Baton Rouge: 1958 (1962). The definitive account; very readable with a specialist's bibliography.

──────. Sword of Pestilence: The New Orleans Yellow Fever Epidemic of 1853, Baton Rouge: 1966. The definitive study on this most tragic of the epidemics.

Dufour, Charles L. Ten Flags in the Wind: The Story of Louisiana, New York: 1967. A fascinating synthesis unfolded with great skill.

──────. The Night the War was Lost, New York, 1960. The work of a New Orleans newspaperman; first-class, readable, controversial chronicle on the importance of Admiral Farragut's victory on April 14, 1862.

Dyer, John P. Tulane: The Biography of a University, 1834-1965, New York: 1966.

Echezabal, Josephine. "The History of the Orleans Public Belt Railroad," MA Thesis, Tulane University (1926).

Everett, Donald I. "Free Persons of Color in New Orleans -- 1803-1865," Tulane University, Ph. D. (1952).

Feibleman, James K. "Literary New Orleans between World Wars," Southern Review, vol. I, no. 3 (New Series: 1965).

Fortier, Alcée. A History of Louisiana, 4 vols., Revised edition by Jo Carrigon, Baton Rouge: 1972. Reprint of a 1904 classic with invaluable editorial work by an accomplished historian, especially useful in medical history; many documents.

Fossier, Albert E. New Orleans: The Glamour Period, 1800-1840, New Orleans: 1957.

Gayarré, Charles E. History of Louisiana, 4 vols., New York: 1866 (Fifth edition, New Orleans: 1965).

Genthe, Arnold. Impressions of New Orleans, a Book of Pictures, New

York: 1926. Strikingly attractive photographs of the city's most charming scenes.

Gottschalk, Louis Moreau. Notes of a Pianist, New York: 1964. Important insights into the creative life of the city by one of its most famous artists.

Griffin, Max L. "A Bibliography of New Orleans Magazines," Louisiana Historical Quarterly, vol. 18, no. 3 (1935).

Griffin, Thomas Kurtz. New Orleans: A Guide to America's Most Interesting City, New York: 1961.

Haas, Edward F. "New Orleans on the Half Shell: The Maestri Era - 1936-46," Louisiana History, vol. 13, no. 3 (1972). An important pioneering study.

Harris, Thomas H. The Story of Public Education in Louisiana, Baton Rouge: 1924.

Hearn, Lafcadio. Creole Sketches, ed. by Charles Hutson, New York: 1924.

Hecht, R. S. Municipal Finances of New Orleans, 1860-1916, New Orleans: 1916.

Heleniak, Roman. "Local Reactions to the Great Depression in New Orleans: 1929-1933," Louisiana History, vol. X (1969).

Hennick, Louis C. and E. Harper Charlton. The Streetcars of Shreveport, 1831-1965, New Orleans: 1965.

Hill, Henry B. and Larry Gara. "A French Traveler's View of Ante-Bellum New Orleans," Louisiana History, vol. I (1960). A useful study of the ideas of the Frenchman, Heinrich Herz, who published his impressions of New Orleans as part of a study of America in the 1860's.

History of the New Orleans Police Department: Benefit of the Police Mutual Benevolent Association of New Orleans, New Orleans: 1900. A rare book; disappointing study but the best so far.

Howe, William Wirt. Municipal History of New Orleans, Baltimore: 1889. A short but useful study in the Johns Hopkins University Studies in History and Political Science (7th series, IV).

Howell, Elmo. "William Faulkner's New Orleans," Louisiana History, no. 7 (1966).

Huber, Leonard V. "Mardi Gras: The Golden Age," American Heritage, vol. 16, no. 2 (February, 1965).

_____. New Orleans, A Pictorial History, New York: 1971. A work that promises to become a modern classic in the tradition of Edwin Jewell's Crescent City Illustrated. Brilliantly edited with a useful bibliography.

_____, and Clarence A. Wagner. The Great Mail: A Postal History of New Orleans, State College, Pennsylvania: 1949.

_____, Samuel Wilson, Jr. and Garland F. Taylor, Louisiana Purchase, New Orleans: 1953.

Inger, Morton. Politics and Reality in an American City: The New Orleans School Crisis of 1960, New York: 1969.

Jackson, Joy. "Bosses and Businessmen - a Gilded Age New Orleans Politics," Louisiana History, no. 5 (1964).

Jackson, Joy J. New Orleans in the Gilded Age: Politics and Urban Progress 1880-1896, Baton Rouge: 1969. An expanded doctorial dissertation by a former staff writer for the Times Picayune.

Jewell, Edwin L. (ed.) Jewell's Crescent City Illustrated, the Commercial Social, Political and General History of New Orleans, Including Biographical Sketches of its Distinguished Citizens, New Orleans: 1873. A collector's item.

Kane, Harnett Thomas. Queen New Orleans, City by the River, New Orleans: 1949. A general view of the history of the city which is tastefully done with beautiful photographs.

Kendall, John Smith. The Golden Age of the New Orleans Theatre, Baton Rouge; New York: 1952. Based on the personal experiences of a late nineteenth century theater-going journalist.

_____. History of New Orleans, 3 vol., New York: 1922. Rare indispensable compilation written with skill and compassion and occasional bias by an eminent journalist.

_____. "Notes on the Criminal History of New Orleans," The Louisiana Historical Quarterly, vol. 34, (1951).

King, Grace Elizabeth. Creole Families of New Orleans, Baton Rouge: 1971. Though a floridly written "literary antique" of the post-Civil War period, it remains a classic in New Orleans social and geneological history.

_____. New Orleans: The Place and People, New York: 1904.

Kmen, Henny A. Music in New Orleans, Baton Rouge: 1966. A beautifully written and historically solid work based on a massive documentation; an excellent cultural history.

Korn, Bertram W. Benjamin Levy: New Orleans Printer and Publisher, Portland, Me.: 1961.

──────. The Early Jew of New Orleans, Waltham, Massachusetts: 1969.

Kraus, John W. William Beer and the New Orleans Libraries, 1891-1927, Chicago: 1952.

Landry, Stuart O. The Battle of Liberty Place: The Overthrow of Carpet-Bag Rule in New Orleans -- September 14, 1874, New Orleans: 1955.

Latrobe, Benjamin Henry. Impressions Respecting New Orleans: Diary and Sketches, 1818-1820. Edited with an Introduction and Note by Samuel Wilson, Jr., New York: 1951. A handsome volume of the work of the English born architect and engineer responsible for the Greek revival in the United States; intelligent and conscientious job of editing.

──────. Journal of Benjamin Henry Latrobe, New York: 1905.

Latrobe, J. H. B. The First Steamboat Voyage on the Western Waters, Baltimore: 1871.

Le Conte, René. "The Germans in Louisiana in the Eighteenth Century." Translated and edited by G. R. Conrad. Louisiana History, vol. 8, no. 1 (1967).

Le Gardeur, René J. Jr. The First New Orleans Theater, 1792-1803, New Orleans: 1963. An excellent monograph.

Lestage, H. Oscar Jr. "The White League in Louisiana and Its Participation in the Reconstruction Riots," Louisiana Historical Quarterly, vol. 18. no. 3 (1935).

Levasseur, A. Lafayette in America in 1824 and 1825 or Journal of Travels in the United States, New York: 1829.

Long, Edith Elliot. Madame Olivier's Mansion: 828 Toulouse, New Orleans: 1965.

Longstreet, Stephen. Sportin' House: New Orleans and the Jazz Story, Los Angeles: 1965.

Lonn, Ella. Reconstruction in Louisiana after 1868, 2 ed., Gloucester, Mass.: 1967.

Louisiana Board of Health Reports, New Orleans: 1857-1909.

Louisiana History Quarterly, New Orleans: 1917-1960. Since 1960, called Louisiana History. Published by the Louisiana Historical Society; key source for study of New Orleans. An attractive Index published in 1965 by Boyd Cruise.

Lyell, Sir Charles. A Second Visit to the United States, 2 vols., New York: 1849. Impressions by the famous English geologist.

Marino, Samuel J. "Early French-Language Newspapers in New Orleans," Louisiana History (1966).

Mathews, Richard I. "New Orleans Revolution of 1768: A Reappraisal," Louisiana Studies, vol. 4, no. 2 (1965).

McCaleb, Walter Flavius. "The Aaron Burr Conspiracy and New Orleans," American Historical Association: Annual Report (1903).

McMurtrie, Douglas Crawford. Early Printing in New Orleans, 1764-1810, New Orleans: 1929. Contains a bibliography of the "issues of the Press" and some documents.

Mitchell, Harry A. "The Development of New Orleans as a Wholesale Center," Louisiana Historical Quarterly, vol. 27, no. 4 (1944).

Moehlenbrok, Arthur Henry. "The German Drama on the New Orleans Stage," Louisiana Historical Quarterly, XXVI (April, 1943).

Morrison, John H. History of American Steam Navigation, New York: 1903.

Moses, Robert. An Arterial Plan for New Orleans, New York: 1946.

Nau, John F. The German People of New Orleans, 1950-1958, Leiden: 1958.

New Orleans City Guide. Federal Writer's Project of the Works Progress Administration, Boston: 1938. Recently reprinted (1952). Still useful source with information on almost everything about New Orleans; many fine photographs.

New Orleans Riots, 1866. House of Representatives, 39th United States Congress. Contains full testimony on riots; a valuable source.

Niehaus, Earl F. The Irish in New Orleans, 1800-1860, Baton Rouge: 1965.

Noble, Stuart G. "Schools in New Orleans During the First Quarter of the 19th Century," Louisiana Historical Quarterly, vol. 14, no. 1 (1931).

O'Conner, Stella. "The Charity Hospital at New Orleans: An Administration and Financial History, 1736-1941," Louisiana Historical Quarterly, vol. 31, no. 1 (1948). Contains an important bibliography.

O'Connor, Thomas. History of the Fire Department of New Orleans, From the Earliest Days to the Present Time, New Orleans: 1895. Rare, of limited value, but fascinating company history.

Parkman, Francis. La Salle and the Discovery of the Great West, Edited by John A. Hawgood, New York: 1962.

Peters, Martha Ann. "The St. Charles Hotel: New Orleans Social Center, 1837-1860," Louisiana History, vol. 1, no. 3, (Summer, 1960).

Phillips, Horace P. "Bonded Debt of New Orleans, 1822-1920," Louisiana Historical Quarterly, vol. 3, no. 4 (1920).

Proctor, Samuel. "Jewish Life in New Orleans, 1718-1806," Louisiana Historical Quarterly, vol. XL, no. 2 (April, 1957).

Reed, Merl E. New Orleans and the Railroad: The Struggle for Commercial Empire, 1830-1860, Baton Rouge: 1966. A condensation and interpretation of important material, well-written; chronicles not only railroads, but the "river psychology" of New Orleans economic interests -- comprehensive bibliography.

Reynolds, Donald E. "The New Orleans Riot of 1866 Reconsidered," Louisiana History, no. 5 (1964).

Reynolds, George M. Machine Politics in New Orleans, New York: 1936. A useful book on the Choctaw Club and New Orleans politics.

Ricciuti, Italo W. New Orleans and Its Environs: The Domestic Architecture, New York: 1938.

Rickey, Emma Cecilia and Evelina O. Kean. The New Orleans Book, New Orleans: 1915.

Rightor, Henry (ed.) Standard History of New Orleans, Chicago: 1900. Still of some value.

Roeder, Robert E. "Merchants of Ante-bellum New Orleans," Explorations in Entrepreneurial History, (April, 1958).

Rose, Al and Edmond Souchon. New Orleans Jazz: A Family Album, Baton Rouge: 1967.

Sala, George Augustus. America Revisited: From the Bay of New York to the Gulf of Mexico, London: 1882.

Samuel, Ray. The Great Days of the Garden District and the Old City of Lafayette, New Orleans: 1961.

Samuel, Ray and Martha Ann. The Uptown River Corner: The Story of

Royal and Bienville, New Orléans: 1964.

Saxon, Lyle. Fabulous New Orleans, New York: 1928. Brings to life the fabulous in New Orleans history; beautifully illustrated and well researched.

Semple, Henry C. The Ursalines of New Orleans, 1727-1925, New York: 1925.

Shgall, Leo. "The First Synagogue in New Orleans," Louisiana Historical Quarterly, vol. 22, no. 2 (1938).

Shugg, Roger Wallace. "The New Orleans General Strike of 1892," Louisiana Historical Quarterly, vol. 21, no. 2 (1938).

Sinclair, Harold. Port of New Orleans, New York: 1942. Still the best treatment; realistic and critical work based on careful research yet entertainingly written.

Smith, Sol. Theatrical Management in the West and South for 30 Years . . . with Anecdotical Sketches, New York: 1868. An unusual source on theatrical history.

Smither, Nelle. A History of the English Theatre in New Orleans, New York: 1967.

Somers, Dale A. "A City on Wheels: The Bicycle Era of New Orleans," Louisiana History, no. 8 (1967).

Somers, Dale Allan. The Rise of Sports in New Orleans, 1850-1900, New Orleans: 1972.

Soule, Leon C. "The Creole -- American Struggle in New Orleans Politics, 1850-1862," Louisiana Historical Quarterly, vol. XL, no. 1 (1957).

_____. The Know Nothing Party in New Orleans: A Reappraisal, Baton Rouge: 1961.

Sterling, David Lee. "New Orleans, 1801: An Account by John Pintard," Louisiana Historical Quarterly, vol. 34, no. 3 (July, 1951).

Stoddart, T. Lathrop. The French Revolution in San Domingo, Boston and New York: 1914.

Szarkowski, John (ed.) E. J. Bellocq: Storyville Portraits, Photographs from the New Orleans Red-Light District, circa 1912. With a preface and prints by Lee Friedlander, New York: 1970. A keyhole look at a segment of New Orleans life.

Tallant, Robert. Mardi Gras, Garden City, New York: 1948.

_____. Voodoo in New Orleans, New York: 1946. A carefully detailed introduction to the subject.

Texada, David. Alejandro O'Reilly and the New Orleans Rebels, Lafayette, La.: 1970. A carefully prepared monograph.

Tinker, Edward Larocque. Creole City; Its Past, Its People, New York: 1953. An anecdotal, accurate and detailed history of New Orleans, written with style and grace.

_____. Lafcadio Hearn's American Days, New York: 1924.

_____. The Palingenesis of Craps, New York: 1933. Published in a limited edition of 400, but an amusing interpretation of New Orleans history if you can find it.

Touchstone, Blake. "Voodoo in New Orleans," Louisiana History, vol. 13 (1972). Based on newspaper accounts from the 1870's and 1880's.

Trollope, Frances. Domestic Manners of the Americans: With a History of Mrs. Trollope's Adventure in America. Edited by Donald Smalley, New York: 1949.

Ugan, Guren and Richard Ugan. Carnival Panorama: New Orleans Mardi Gras Medals and Krewes, 1884-1965, New Orleans: 1966.

Vetter, Ernest G. Fabulous Frenchtown: The Story of the Famous Quarter of New Orleans, Washington: 1955. Essentially a guide book; good photographs.

Voss, Louis. Presbyterianism in New Orleans and Adjacent Points, New Orleans: 1931.

Waldo, J. Curtis. History of the Carnival in New Orleans from 1857 to 1882, New Orleans: 1882.

Waring, George E. Jr. Report of the Social Statistics of Cities, Part II: The Southern and Western States, Washington, D. C.: 1887. An invaluable source with a long historical section by the eminent writer, George W. Cable.

Warmoth, Henry Clay. War, Politics, and Reconstruction: Stormy Days in Louisiana, New York: 1930.

Warner, Charles Dudley. Studies in the South and West, London: 1890. A travel report by an Englishman who was in New Orleans during the Exposition of 1885.

Whitaker, Arthur Preston. The Mississippi Question, 1795-1802, A Study on Trade, Politics, and Diplomacy, New York: 1934.

_____. The Spanish-American Frontier: 1783-1795, 2nd. ed., Gloucester, Mass.: 1962.

Williams, Robert W. Jr. "Martin Behrman and New Orleans Civic Development, 1904-1920," Louisiana History, no. 2. (1961).

Williams, T. Harry, "The Politics of the Longs," Georgia Review, Spring, 1961.

Wilson, Neill C. and Frank J. Taylor. Southern Pacific: The Roaring Story of a Fighting Railroad, New York: 1952.

Wilson, Samuel Jr. A Guide to Architecture of New Orleans, 1699-1959, New York: 1959 (Gretna, La.: 1971). First of a series of volumes with a scholarly text and excellent illustrations.

_____. The Capuchin School in New Orleans, 1725, New Orleans: 1961.

_____. The Vieux Carré New Orleans: Its Plan, Its Growth, Its Architecture, Washington, D. C.: 1968.

_____, and Leonard V. Huber. The Basilica on Jackson Square and Its Predecessors, 1729-1965, New Orleans: 1965.

_____, and Leonard V. Huber. The Cabildo on Jackson Square, New Orleans: 1970.

_____, Leonard V. Huber and Abbaye A. Gorin. The St. Louis Cemeteries of New Orleans, New Orleans: 1963.

Winters, John D. The Civil War in Louisiana, Baton Rouge: 1963.

Yerburg, Grace H. "Concert Music in Early New Orleans," Louisiana Historical Quarterly, vol. L, no. 2 (1951).

Young, Perry. The Mistick Krewe: Chronicles of Comus and His Kin, New Orleans: 1931.

NAME INDEX

Adler, D.H., 27
Alciatore, Antoine, 16
Alexander III, Crown Prince of Russia, 26
Almonester y Roxas, Don, 17
Anderson, Adolf, 22
Audubon, Jean Jacques, 12, 13

Banks, Gen. N.P., 24
Banks, Thomas, 14
Barnum, P.T., 19, 20
Beaujolais, Comte, 7
Behan, W.J., 30
Behrman, Martin, 35, 38
Benjamin, Judah P., 23
Bolivar, Simon, 50
Boré, Etienne de, 7
Boré, Jean, 24
Bowen, Andy, 33
Braud, A.M., 4
Brown, James, 13
Bunche, Dr. Ralph J., 47
Burke, Jack, 33
Burr, Aaron, 10
Butler, Gen. Benjamin F., 23

Caldwell, James H., 13
Calvo, Casa, 8
Capdeville, Paul, 34
Carnegie, Andrew, 36
Carondelet, Baron de, 6
Cavagnal, Pierre, Marquis de Vaudreuil, 3
Cavelier, Robert, Sieur de La Salle, 1
Cenas, Blaise, 9
Charles III of Spain, 5
Charles IV of Spain, 5
Charles, Robert, 34
Charlevoix, Father, 1, 2
Claiborne, William C.C., 8
Clark, George Rogers, 5
Cleveland, President, 33
Cobb, A.A. 47, 48
Cohn, Joseph, 18
Conway, John R., 25
Conway, Rev. T.W., 25

Corbett, James L., 33
Crossman, Abdil Daily, 18

Darwin, Charles, 26
Davis, Jefferson, 23
Davis, John, 12
Davis, Governor, 51
Degas, Edgar, 26
DeGaulle, Pres. Charles, 51
Delgado, Isaac, 36
DePalma, Ralph, 36
DeSoto, Hernando, 1
Donizetti, 22
Dorgenois, LeBreton, 11
Duclot, Louis, 6

Eads, James B., 28
Eisenhower, Pres. Dwight D., 49
Eustis, James Biddle, 33

Farragut, David E., 23
Faulkner, William, 38
Fitzpatrick, John, 32
Flanders, Benjamin Franklin, 26
Flower, Walter C., 33
Freccia, M., 44
Freret, William, 17

Gaillot, Mrs. B.J., 54
Gallier, James Sr., 20
Gallier and Dakins, 14
Galvez, Don Bernardo de, 5
Garrison, District Attorney James, 54, 55, 56, 57
Gayarré, Charles, 24
Gayosa, Don Manuel de Lemos, 8
Genois, Charles, 16
Gottshalk, Louis Moreau, 13
Grant, Captain, 13
Grant, Gen. Ulysses S., 29
Grétry, André, 7
Guillotte, J. Valsin, 30

Harding, Sen. Warren, 38
Hall, W. Covington, 35
Heath, Edward, 25
Hebert, Congressman Edward, 50

Hemingway, Ernest, 38
Hennessy, David C., 32
Henry, O. (William Sidney Porter), 33
Hirt, Al, 57
Hitler, Adolf, 44
Hortner and Fenner, 27
Houston, Sam, 18
Howard, Charles T., 25

Irby, William Ratcliffe, 37

Jackson, Gen. Andrew, 11, 17

Kaye, Danny, 56
Kefauver, Senator Estes, 48
Kellogg, Gen. William Pitt, 27
Kendall, George Wilkins, 16, 18
Kennedy, President John F., 53, 54, 55, 56, 57
Kerlerec, Louis Billouard de, 4
Kirby-Smith, Gen. Edmund, 24
Klaw and Erlanger, 34
Kohn, Aaron M., 48, 52

Lafayette, General, 13
Landrieu, Moon, 57, 58
Latrobe, Benjamin H., 12, 13
Laussat, Pierre, 8
Law, John, 1
Le Blond de la Tour, Pierre, 2
Lee, Robert E., 26, 30
Leeds, Charles, 27
Leis, John L., 21
Lemoyne, Jean Baptiste (Sieur de Bienville), 1
Lemoyne, Pierre (Sieur d'Iberville), 1
Lesdiguieres, Duchesse de, 1
Lind, Jenny, 20
Long, Huey P., 40, 41, 42, 43
Lopez, Gen. Narisco, 32
Louis, Jean, 3
Louis XV of France, 1
Louis Philippe of France, 8
Lumsden, Col. Francis Asbury, 16

McCartney, August, 11
McDonogh, John, 17
McKinley, President William, 34
Maestri, Robert S., 42, 43, 44
Marigny, Bernard, 14
Marigny, Pierre de, 8
Martin, François Xavier, 13
Mather, James, 10
Mestach, George, 36
Milhet, Jean, 4
Milton, John, 21
Miro, Don Estevan, 5
Monro, John T., 22
Monroe, President James, 13
Monroe, John T., 24
Montegut, Joseph Edgard, 17
Montpensier, Duc, 7
Mora, Policeman, 34
Morales, Intendant, 8
Morial, F.N., 55
Morphy, Paul, 22
Morris, John A., 25
Morrison, Le Lesseps S., 45, 46, 47, 48, 49, 50, 51, 52
Moscoso, Luis, 1
Mowry, John, 9, 12

Napoleon I, 8
Newcomb, Joseph Le Monnier, 31

O'Keefe, Arthur J., 39, 40
O'Reilly, Gen. Alexander, 4
Orleans, Philippe Duc de, 1
Oswald, Lee Harvey, 54

Patti, Adelina, 22
Patton, Isaac W., 28
Pauger, Adrien de, 2
Penalvert, Don Louis de, 7
Perier, Etienne de, 2
Pierce, President, 20
Pilsbury, Edward, 27
Pitot, James, 9
Pius VI, Pope, 6
Pius IX, Pope, 19
Polk, President, 18
Pollack, Oliver, 5

Pontalba, Baroness Micaela, 17
Portevent, Eliza Jane, 32
Poydras, Julian, 11
Prieur, Denis, 13, 17

Reid, Sheriff H., 48
Richardson, Henry Hobson, 16
Rillieux, Norbert, 18
Robb, James, 22
Robin, C.C., 16
Roffignac, Joseph, 12
Roosevelt, President Franklin Delano, 43
Roosevelt, Nicholas, 11
Roosevelt, President Theodore, 35
Rossini, Gioacchino, 22
Rummel, Archbishop Joseph F., 52

Sacedo, Don Juan Manuel de, 8
Schiro, Victor, 52, 53, 54, 57
Sedella, Padre Antonio de, 5
Shakespeare, Joseph A., 29, 31
Shaw, C.L., 56
Shreve, Henry M., 11
Slidell, John, 18, 23
Soulé, Pierre, 20
Story, Sidney (Mrs. Mary Hayden Green), 33, 34
Strich, Gerard, 22
Sullivan, John L., 33

Tabary, Louis, 6
Taft, President William Howard, 36

Taylor, Gen. Zachary, 18
Thackeray, William Makepeace, 21
Toledano, B.C., 57
Tonti, Henri de, 1
Touro, Judah, 8, 12
Treme, Claude, 10
Tulane, Paul, 30
Turner, Bishop, 34

Ulloa, Don Antonio de, 4
Unzaga, Don Luis de, 5

Vaudreuil, Marquis Pierre Cavagnac de, 3
Villeneuve, Le Blance, 3

Walmsley, T. Semmes, 40, 41, 42
Ward, C.R., 56
Warren, Chief Justice Earl, 55
Waterman, Charles M., 21
Watkins, John, 9
Webb and Knapp, 49
Wilde, Oscar, 30
Wilder, Thornton, 38
Wilkinson, Gen. James, 8
Wiltz, Louis A., 26
Wimberly, S., 45
Wood, A.T., 19
Wright, Judge J. Skelly, 50

Yarrut, Judge, 47

Zatarain, C.C., 47
Zeckendorf, William, 49